Spaghetti

Junction

An

Italian in

Walsall

By

Antonio

Longhi

IN 2010 I AM SINGING VOLARE ON THE
STAGE OF ALDRIDGE COMMUNITY ASSOCIA
TION. I AM PRETENDING TO BE THE
SINGER DOMENICO₃MODUGNO, HENCE
MOUSTACHE AND WIG

Contents

Chapter One

Singing

I was born in Rome and at age eleven I was sent to a fee-paying school run by very strict priests who were beating us, often for no reason at all. But they were good teachers. There was a redeeming factor about the 'Pio IX 'school, it was located on the Aventine hill in a fantastic villa. But the main factor that stopped us boys from escaping and enrol in the Foreign Legion where discipline would have been more relaxed, was that literally next door to our school was the 'Accademia Nazionale di Balletto 'where future ballet stars were learning their craft.

Some days our school and their school finished at the same time and a huge scrum of male and female bodies happened in the small square outside the schools.

But I am digressing, so let us go back to singing.

At the end of the school year us boys had to perform for our parents, and each one of us performed according to his ability, after a test I was chosen to sing in the choir of Aida (only the choral part was sung, not the entire Opera). I never learnt to read or play music, but I only had to hear a tune once and I could sing it. My family did not buy a TV set till I was a teenager, so in the evening we would listen to Opera on the radio, that is why I knew already words and music of most Operas. I enjoyed singing so much that I sang at every possible occasion, in the school choir, at parties, at birthdays or weddings.

Once I moved to the UK my singing career took off. I had married an English woman and my English family did not like my willingness to sing in public, because they found it very embarrassing, but I could not help it, if somebody sung I felt the urge to join in. About thirty years ago we all went to the Alexandra theatre in Birmingham where the Russian Army Ensemble was performing dancing and singing, when a tenor started singing 'O sole mio' I joined him in singing, but I was immediately silenced by elbows digging in my stomach (to a much lesser extent it still happens thirty years later).

The show ended, and the audience proceeded to the multi storey car park, and there I announced to my family that I could not wait any more and I started singing 'O sole mio '. My family immediately took cover behind concrete pillars and cars, so pretending not to know me, but all the ladies and gentlemen in their fine evening dresses gave me a standing ovation (it had to be standing, no sets in the car park).

At the time one of my neighbours called Horace sung in the Sheffield Male Voice Choir. Occasionally I went to his flat and over a cup of tea we would rehearse the next concert programme, and I would teach correct Italian pronunciation. Over the years I went to nearly all their performances, so learning their tunes, and in the interval, I would sing with them. I now must introduce another character, George. George had landed at Anzio with the British troops in 1943, the year I was born. We became friends because of the Italian connection. Every year the choir would have dinner in a restaurant and invited friends and family. At the end of the meal the choir would go on the stage and sing for their relatives and friends. One year George was walking towards the stage, he stopped by me and asked me to get up and sing with the choir. I retorted that I was not prepared, I had not rehearsed with them. He gesticulating, replied that when the conductor goes like this you start singing and when he does that you stop. I asked why, since it was so easy, the choir was rehearsing for two hours every Monday evening. He said 'I know you can sing and you owe it to me to sing with us, because if it were not for myself and many more like me who fought for the freedom of your country, everyone in Italy would now be speaking German '. At that point I had to get up and go on the stage.

I was standing between George and Horace. Of course, I could sing their repertoire and I was enjoying singing, when I could hear a voice behind me who was whispering 'Spaghetti, pizza, tortellini............' I turned, and it was the choir bursar who told me 'Antonio I wanted to make you feel relaxed, and these are the only Italian words I know' 'I replied 'Thanks but for God's sake will you shut up because your whispering is confusing me.'

Alas my two very good friends George and Horace are now singing in the angels' choir, and I had the privilege to sing at their funerals.

The occasion for my international debut was the marriage of my second son Andrea in Szeged, Hungary, with beautiful Joanna

Lumley lookalike Katalin. Unknown to me the best man, during his speech said, " We all know how much you enjoy singing, so we have prepared a surprise for you, will you sing a duet with a soprano who has sung at La Scala in Milan, the Metropolitan in New York ………." At last I could sing to my family on their request!! I proposed to sing the aria La' ci darem la mano from Don Giovanni by Mozart. We both sang it well and a distant relative of the bride who was the official photographer recorded it on video tape. I also remember that this guy had taken a shine to my wife, and I made it obvious that he had gone too far (in reality he had gone too near). Years later I decided to transfer the video tape on DVD. But the chap who did the video tape had edited it cancelling all the singing, I suppose because he did not like my reaction to the advances he made to my wife. So, the world will never know how good I was.

At this stage in my singing career something unfortunate happened. A routine sinus operation went terribly wrong and the surgeon left a 10p big hole in my septum bone, but he did not tell me. I felt worse than before the operation, I kept bleeding for months, then he discharged me saying there was nothing else he could do for me (in fact he had done too much because I was not born with a hole in my septum.) I asked my GP for a second opinion and was referred to an ENT specialist at the Queen Elizabeth hospital in Birmingham. This specialist showed me on X-ray the hole in my nose and could not believe I had not been told and been discharged. He told me he would operate me again in order to plug the hole. But when I woke up after the operation the surgeon told me he had not been able to plug the hole because the NHS did not provide big enough plugs. I could hardly sing at all and singing is one of the loves of my life. When I sing at full voice empty my lungs I feel a sense of euphoria and wellbeing that I can only compare to the joy of love making. But I never give up, so I went privately to a specialist in London Harley street. He gave me a thorough check, and at the end he told that my nose was beyond repair, and I would never sing again because my vocal chords had been damaged.

With this news I returned home which was and is Walsall, West Midlands. But I never give up, so a few years later I go on the internet and went privately to another ENT specialist, Mr. Simmons, this time in Walsall. When I mentioned the name of the specialist I had seen in London he told me he was the best in the UK and that he had been his teacher at University. He decided to operate me again on the NHS to save me money, in order to improve my condition. When I asked him how much it was for his consultation he replied 'Mr. Longhi you owe me nothing, I want you to reconcile with the medical profession 'I will never forget that. A couple of months later he operated me, I woke up and there was no bleeding from my nose! The damage limitation was successful, but I could not sing any more for a couple of hours on the stage but given the right conditions i.e. dry and warm weather. I could still sing a few solos. And sing I did.

I had become a member and committee member of Walsall U3A (University of the third age). A couple of years ago I also became the speaker secretary, and in that capacity, I have to book, pay, introduce, and look after during their performances speakers and entertainers. A week ago, for our Christmas celebration I had booked Keith Slater, a singer specialising in performing as Frank Sinatra. I usually have a chat with them while they are getting ready and I mentioned that I used to sing. Having noticed my thick Italian accent, he said 'I bet you are a tenor ', and to prove he was right I sung a few lines of Nessun Dorma. Usually I introduce the performers, but he had asked to introduce himself; during his introduction he mentioned that Walsall U3A was blessed with having as speaker secretary a renowned tenor. When he finished his very good performance I replied that I was not aware of being famous, and to reciprocate his compliment I mentioned that I had listened to Frank Sinatra singing live in Las Vegas, and that in my opinion there was not that much difference between old blue eyes' voice and his voice.

About five years ago I have met by a very strange coincidence the Welsh professional tenor Richard Lloyd Owen. We were talking on my door step when he asked if I were Italian and when I replied yes he exclaimed "I sing Italian Opera in Italian and only the Italians and the Welsh can sing! "I invited him in and we sung together, that was the beginning of a friendship still lasting today. He invited me to his home for one of his rehearsals and asked me to correct his Italian pronunciation. After singing an aria he asked my opinion and I said it was great singing, but he was not happy with it, so he sung it again and recorded it, then he put earpieces on me and made me listen again. Even my uneducated ear could tell that he had improved it by 2/3 %. And that meant that he was at the top of his profession. I was amazed when I heard him sing how beautiful his voice was and wandered why he had not made it to a big Opera House. But that is another story.

Since I could not sing any more for a long time, in order to keep in touch with music and singing, about two years ago I started the Opera group within Walsall U3A. Once a month I organise a concert and when Richard is available he sings live Opera arias and he brings with him a pianist, a soprano and a mezzo soprano. Sometimes these singers are his students because he also teaches singing at Birmingham Conservatoire and privately. Other times I take my Opera group to theatres where Opera is performed or to Opera singers shows.

Last year I took my Opera group to the Grand theatre in Wolverhampton where Leslie Garrett was singing. At the end of her performance she gave the audience the opportunity of questions and answers, and I was dying to grab the mike. When I did I congratulated on her perfect Italian pronunciation (even if I was ten yards away I thought she blushed). She said she was happy that an Italian did appreciate her singing and mentioned that the Italian language was the most melodious for singing. Naturally I agreed with her and said that a music genius like Mozart knew that his Operas would have been perfect if sung in Italian rather than German. So, he enrolled an Italian librettist, Lorenzo Da Ponte, to write the librettos for his Operas, the only exception being The

Magic Flute. At that moment I started singing my favourite aria La'
ci darem la mano from Mozart's Don Giovanni, and she carried on
singing the soprano part from the stage. Therefore, in my singing
career CV I could mention that I have sung with Leslie Garrett,
although I from the audience and she from the stage. But that is a
mere technicality.

One day last year I was in my home giving an Italian
language lesson, when the telephone rung. It was my friend Victor
who needed a favour. "Antonio a few days ago my brother-in-law
died ...." "Oh dear, I am sorry, but what has it got to do with me?"
"Well .... you see I had booked a singer to sing at the funeral, but
he can't make it........." "Book another one then" "There is no time
because the funeral is today at 1230 at Streetly
crematorium.........could you come and sing?"

It was 1100. "Victor give me the titles of the hymns and I will
do my best". I finished the lesson quickly, went on the Internet and
heard the two hymns being sung, printed the words and raced to the
funeral. The funeral cortege had not arrived yet, but the organist was
there. I explained the situation and asked him to have a rehearsal
before the funeral arrived, we did it just in time. I sung the hymns,
then excused myself and left. The day after Victor rings my door
bell. "Antonio thank you very much, you saved the day and sung
beautifully, my sister is so grateful that she has asked me to pay
you." "But Victor, I did it because you are a friend, and when I ask
you to make a DVD when I sing, you do it and do not ask for money,

also I am an amateur and have never accepted money for singing, which I enjoy anyway." "In that case accept this man bag I bought when we were in Rome on holiday." And that was an offer I could not refuse.

I am also a member of the National Trust, and a couple of years ago the Walsall branch organised a coach trip to Stafford Castle to watch Othello. Before the play started a member of staff was warming the audience by playing the guitar, and may be because I look Italian, he came by me and started playing "O' sole mio." I could not resist such a provocation/invitation, and although at the time I was sitting between the National Trust chairman and his lady on my left, and the U3A chairman and his lady on my right, I stood up and sung one of my best "O sole mio", second only to my performance in the Alexandra theatre car park, when my vocal chords were still in pristine condition. At the end of the play the audience started walking towards their coaches and cars, when a lady walks towards me, hugs me and kisses me. I thought she had fallen in love with my singing, my Mediterranean good looks, and my natural charm. But I could smell alcohol from her breath "Have you had one too many?" I asked, "I have had many too many." My romance hopes dashed, I escorted her to her coach where we promised each other to meet again, same place same time next year, and then proceeded to find my coach. My singing exploit had not passed entirely unnoticed, and in the next issue of the National Trust magazine there was a comment on the trip to Stafford Castle. "The play was excellent, but Antonio singing O sole mio stole the show."

Another story related to singing, even if it was not my singing, was when my beloved daughter Laura organised a trip to La Scala in Milan for Turandot, and Turandot is where the famous aria "Nessun Dorma" became world famous when the three tenors sung it in the Caracalla Baths in Rome for the first time during the football world cup "Italia '90" (I was there). It was done as a present for my 72nd birthday. She could not book two seats together, but before the interval texted me that during the interval we would drink a bottle of champagne together. The interval arrives, and I go down to the foyer, but we could not find each other. Turandot ends, and we finally meet in the foyer, and holding an empty champagne bottle she hugs me and whispers "Dad I had to drink all the champagne myself."

She was happy to say the least, so I hailed a taxi and we went back to the hotel. The bar in the hotel was still open so I told Laura to grab a seat while I was getting a drink for myself. At the bar there was a young man who started chatting to me, it transpired he was a Brazilian solicitor and had come with a Brazilian party for Turandot. I also have a Brazilian daughter-in-law apart from a Hungarian one, so I exchanged a few pleasantries and carried on with my drink. Then he wanted to buy me a drink and I politely accepted; he also asked me if the beautiful girl I came with was my daughter and I replied affirmatively. It could be because of the alcohol but suddenly I find myself singing "Cielito Lindo" in Spanish with a Brazilian solicitor and a Polish barman. Then when the Brazilian started admiring the silk waist jacket of my tuxedo and touched it, I realised it was time for a sharp exit. In the morning Laura and I were having breakfast when I mentioned that the Brazilian guy thought she was beautiful "But dad did you not realise that he was gay and was trying to get to you through me?" It was as if a thunderbolt had struck me, thinking back I remembered he had no beard to speak of and his behaviour was peculiar to say the least. She was right. It was a sad day for me because I realised that in my second youth I was still pulling, but I was pulling the wrong gender.

I had decided not to write any more about my singing for fear of boring you, but overnight another episode flashed back. I was holidaying in Corfu', and one evening I went to reception and asked about a place where I could enjoy Greek music and dancing, the Zorba the Greek stuff. I was given an address in the middle of the mountains (I was staying in a seaside hotel) with the recommendation that since I had already dined in the hotel, I should buy drinks or a snack, since the place where I was going did not charge an entry fee. I thanked her, booked a taxi and off I went. It was a hotel/restaurant with a dancing hall and a stage. I duly asked for drinks and relaxed in anticipation of a good evening. The show started with a fantastic solo performance of the Greek guitar, if I remember correctly called the bassoki, then dancers in national costume came and the audience was asked to join in.

Having enjoyed the dancing, I went back to my table, and then a blonde attractive youngish woman came to my table and asked me "Why are you on your own?" "Because I was hoping to meet a beautiful Greek lady to dance with, but surely you are not Greek, there are not that many Greek ladies blond with blue eyes." "That is because I am a Yorkshire lass, and by the way I own this place." "Pleased to meet you, and I am a Roman centurion on holiday. Would you like me to entertain your guest with my singing?" "That would be great, go to the pianist and ask if he knows the songs you want to sing." I went and the first thing the pianist asked was "In what key do you sing?" "The only keys I know are car keys, door keys, etc. I would like to sing Arrivederci Roma and Volare. You play, and I will sing." He gave me a puzzled look and nodded. The place was full of Australian students on a Europe discovery trip, Russians because of the proximity to their country and because they were becoming rich after the collapse of the USSR, and lastly of Hungarians. As I have mentioned before I am the proud father-in-law of a Hungarian Joanna Lumley look alike, and since I know a little Hungarian I exchanged a few words with the Hungarians, then I went to the Russians and did the same (I have done a short Russian Language course at the then called Wolverhampton Polytechnic), the Australians were already past their sell by date because of the amount of alcohol they had already drunk. When my time came, I grabbed the mike, signalled the pianist to start and sung Arrivederci Roma, followed by Volare. I explained mainly to the Australians that they were too young (and drunk) to remember Volare, which became an international number one when it won the European song festival in 1962. It was originally sung by Domenico Modugno, but it had had dozens of versions, including

17

mine which they were going to hear. I explained that when I raised my arms the audience should join me in singing Oh Oh. They all loved it and I received a long applause. The Yorkshire lass approached me, but I had the time to tell her still holding the mike "Now that I have entertained your guests, the least you can do is to waive my bill." "Oh no. I can't do that."

I went back to my table and realised that 12 midnight was fast approaching and like Cinderella I had to go back on my pumpkin at 12 midnight because that is when my taxy was coming to get me. It was a dead shame because the singing, the dancing, the music and the drinking was still at full blast. I went to the cashier and paid my bill. As I was leaving the premises the Yorkshire lass run after me and called me. I turned, and she gave me two bottles of Ouzo, explaining that she could not waive my bill in public because all the drunken Australians would grab the mike, blurt out a few notes and then expect not to pay their bills. I kissed her goodnight and went out where my pumpkin was waiting. There were a few Australians fagging and drinking "Hi Antonio you sung very well mate......." I waved to them and got into the taxi. I know it is hard to believe, but that night out singing was the highlight of my Corfu' holiday, not the sunshine, the beaches, the food and wine. That night is what I will remember forever because I enjoyed the singing, the company, the atmosphere and made a few people happy.

Chapter Two

The Grange

The Grange is a 104 seats theatre situated within Walsall's Arboretum Park. It was built during the last war as a hangar for small aircrafts, and in the early 50's was transformed in a theatre. There are two amateur companies who alternate every month and I am amazed at what they can do on a very small stage. I remember for The Railways Children they managed to have a train running on tracks. But the play that I remember most was a professional performance of The History Boys. I had just seen the film, but the actors performed as well as those in the film. This one and the Aldridge Youth Theatre, 145 seats and on average a play every fortnight is all that Walsall offers as theatres. At the moment The Grange has been undergoing a thorough refurbishment and has been closed since July, it will reopen in September 2018.

I have been going regularly every month for many years and the managers of both companies know that I want to seat on row g seat 7, because it is the front row aisle, and apart from being four yards from the stage I do not have to get up every time somebody wants to come in or go out. One day I was sitting down in seat G7 reading the programme when a young and a not so young woman arrive and the older woman seats by me, looks at me and tells the younger one "You had better sit by this man because he has a sparkle in his eyes". And they exchanged seats. I started chatting with them and it transpired that they are mother and daughter, and to this day I do not understand what the mother saw in a middle-aged bold gentleman reading the programme. In talking, Janet (the younger one) told me she wanted to learn Italian, I told her that I did teach Italian and promptly gave her my business card. The play started and the mother showered me with biscuits, chocolates and sweets till I had to politely decline. During the interval of the play in order to thank the mum I got up and kissed her, then recognising the woman next to the mum as a friend kissed her too and so on till I arrived at the last chair and "I am sorry, but I do not know you" and she replied, "Oh that does not matter" and offered her cheek to me. Having finished the row I stood erect and noticed that lots of ladies in the back of the theatre were waving and shouting "Me too, over here!" Unfortunately, the curtain went up. Janet became my student and we still are friends, you will meet her again in another chapter.

In another occasion I was as usual sitting in G7 and the play was Calendar Girls. Of course, G7 on occasions like this has an extra advantage which was evident to friends behind me, because during the interval they start calling me a dirty old man, and my protestations that I always sit in G7 were met with laughter. A short digression about Calendar Girls.

Many years ago, the then president of Walsall U3A Lilian asked me seriously "I have noticed that 70/80 % of our members are female, what can we do to attract more males?" I replied with a twinkle in my eyes (Janet's mum was right!) "What is that men like?" "Well I am not sure…" "But women of course, and we got plenty of them, and after women football." "So, what are you suggesting?" "That we advertise our ladies by making a Walsall U3A Calendar Girls calendar, the WI did it, why not Walsall U3A? Which we can justify by donating profits to a charity. It could be as chaste as the committee wishes. Then I could start a football group." I thought and still think that it was a good idea, but only the football group was approved, and to think that I had already found January and February models!!

Chapter Three

Travels

Brazil

Since my Muse is Bill Bryson I must write about my travels, Bill and I are both foreigners living in the UK (he not any more) and we look at some British habits in awe. For instance, when they eat the majority of Brits use the fork with the bend down and pile their peas on it and of course they fall, and they patiently using the knife pile it on again. It is a painstakingly effort, while the rest of the world uses the fork as a shovel, otherwise you may as well use chopsticks. I have asked to an erudite friend of mine the reason for this absurdity, and he told me that from the middle ages to not that long ago, the servants used the fork properly, while the nobility upside down. I am open to more suggestions. Another peculiarity is that the Brits in keeping with the stiff upper lip never disclose their feelings, using sentences like "Not too bad" and "It could be worse".

I had been to Brazil when I was working for Alitalia, the Italian Airline, using my worldwide free tickets, but this book is about what happened to me after my arrival in UK in 1988. In 2005 we received an invitation to spend a holiday in Mossoro', the native town of my daughter-in-law Andrea. Mossoro' is situated near the equator and it receives exactly 12 hours of sunshine and 12 hours of darkness. We landed at a city called Natal, named after Christmas day when Vasco de Gama landed there. We stayed a few days in a hotel by the sea. We used to have breakfast outside under a canopy of banana leaves, and multicoloured tropical birds would fly by us to eat the crumbs. It was fiercely hot, over 40c, but there was always a very strong breeze and it was dry heat; therefore, you perceived a much cooler temperature. So, yours truly the second day decided not to wear any sun protection and burnt terribly. Walking in the streets of Natal I noticed that the Brazilian ladies sported open umbrellas, not parasols but rain brollies, to protect their skin. Andrea's family had provided us with a car so that we could drive to Mossoro'. It was a long drive along a motorway, and I noticed police cars on the motorway and at the petrol stations. I asked why there was so much police about, and apparently drivers are killed nearly every day in ambushes by people so poor they literally have nothing to lose. Along the motorway I spotted the houses of these desperados, four sticks and a sheet of plastic on top. No doors, walls, nothing. As we were driving on, the terrain was becoming drier and drier, almost a desert. At last we arrived. The house had individual air conditioning in every room, a swimming pool in the centre, and in the morning a lady cleaner/cook/dogsbody would arrive and cooked breakfast usually an enormous amount of food. In the evening she would call a taxi, a motorbike, and went home.

I was in the habit that as soon as the sun appeared at 0600, would go in the pool, get out for breakfast, then get dressed and went into town. Andrea's sister, Sandra, was working for an Italian chap who had emigrated penniless from Cordenons in the Veneto region a long time ago. Mister Giusti had made a fortune and was the owner of several factories in Brazil, and when he heard that fellow Italians were in town, invited us nearly every day to have lunch with him in the Hotel Thermas. He would treat us for the pleasure of speaking Italian. Thermas in Brazilian means Spa and many years ago there were oil wells instead of an hotel in that area. When the oil dried hot water filled the vacuum. An entrepreneur had built the hotel and swimming pools using the naturally hot water. After lunch we would sunbathe and swim. One day mister Giusti organised a trip for us to a salt factory. In the morning his driver picked us up and drove us to the factory. It was situated by the sea where massive pumps would pump sea water in a dozen pools, where in a few days the sun would evaporate the water and leave salt. The roads between the pools and to the factory were made of salt. When the water had evaporated completely a lorry would collect the salt and take it to the factory where it was cleaned, ground and packaged ready to be sent all over Brazil. We were breathing salt dust all the time and we were very thirsty, so we were taken to a weather station by the pools. The water we drunk from coolers was most welcome, I noticed a rain chart on a wall and read it: January rain 0 mm, February 0 mm, March 0 mm, April 0.3 mm, May 0 mm, June 0.2 mm, July 0 mm, August 0 mm and so on. We thanked the manager of the weather station and drove home.

The next day we went to have dinner in a churrascheria, churrasco in Portuguese means steak, and it was an enormous steak house. On arrival you could choose a starter from a huge variety of vegetables, then the waiters would start serving chunks of meat of any animal, two or four legged, that had ever roamed on earth, and likewise of birds. The only meat not on the menu was dodo and dinosaur. There was no point in telling the waiters "No thank you, I have had enough", because they would not take no for an answer. If you want to try this experience there is a churrascheria in Birmingham Mailbox. But what really got on my nerves was that at the end of that meat orgy I noticed a leaflet on the table "There are thirty million Brazilians dying of starvation, so please eat all the food we serve you" as if gorging ourselves would help the starving Brazilians !!The evening after we went to have dinner at a restaurant owned by one of Andrea's brothers and we were served normal portions of food, we were sitting al fresco and there were children hanging around dressed as if they were rehearsing for Oliver. We were told not to give them any money because they would give it to their parents who would use it to buy drugs and alcohol. Instead we left some food on our dishes and when we got up they went to it as locusts would.

And now meet Fernando, Andrea's brother larger than life character. Fernando was in his 40's and in his youth had been a professional footballer, thus acquiring a decent amount of money, which he invested it in real estate and a souvenir shop. First, we went to the souvenir shop, so small that you had to breathe in before entering and out when you left. He would make a lot of money from that place. Then he took us to an American style ranch or fazenda according to where you came from. There he became a cow boy and performed for us various stunts like lassoing cows and so on. It was like watching a far west film, but this was real life. Jolly Fernando had to work hard because I do not remember how many times he got married, but I know he had fathered a considerable number of children and loved them all and looked after them like a doting father.

One day we drove along the seashore till we arrived at a hotel by the beach. It was owned by Hermann, a German who had emigrated to Brazil a few years earlier. Over dinner Hermann told us why he had moved to Brazil. He owned a company in Germany, but did not like the long harsh winters, getting up in the morning and scraping ice from the car windscreen etc. One day like St. Paul on the road to Damascus, he saw the light, sold his company, booked a ticket for Brazil, and with that money bought a slice of Brazilian jungle that included a hotel, restaurant, and a beach. There he married a gorgeous Brazilian woman and started a family. I do sympathise with him a lot. Bear in mind that everything in Brazil is cheaper than in Europe, also the exchange rate was 1 to 4 so he would get 4 cruzeiros for every German Mark. The day after I had breakfast, then went for a stroll on the beach and found Hermann lying on a hammock he had placed near the entrance of his hotel. I greeted him and asked what he was doing there

"I am working "

Working?"

"Working yes, I am strategically placed and if a customer comes through the open door I get up and serve him, then I get back on the hammock". And this used to be a very hard-working person working to German ethos! Other mornings he would work fishing on the beach and at the same time keeping an eye to the hotel. One day he asked me if I liked pizza which is like asking a German if he likes his beer and sauerkrauts. Of course, I said yes. In the evening Hermann's Brazilian chef produced the best pizza I have ever eaten anywhere in the world. This lifestyle affected my son Marco so much that he seriously thought of doing a Hermann. I would like to add that since 2005 living conditions in Brazil have improved considerably.

Austria

Salzburg

Five years ago, our son Christian thought that I and my wife Jo deserved a holiday and treated us to one in Salzburg. Our hotel was located just outside the city centre which is all pedestrianised. Salzburg is an amazing place; the centre is intact, and all the buildings keep the original Austrian style. Salzburg is also the birthplace of my hero Wolfgang Amadeus Mozart, and if you did not know you would soon be aware of it because you land at Mozart airport, all the shops sell Mozart souvenirs such as Mozart chocolate figurines, Mozart harpsichords, the list is endless. In the Morning my wife and I would have breakfast in the small kiosk just across the road. We usually had a gigantic sausage in a roll watered down with a beer for myself and a coffee for Jo. Every morning the only other client was an elderly gentleman wearing the typical Austrian national dress, socks to the knees, short trousers to the knees, a shirt and a waist coat, a hat with a feather. He did what the Brits do when they go to their local pub, have a drink or two, chat to the owner and other clients, which meant Jo and me. He was a feast for your eyes, and I asked if I could take a picture of him; he gave an enthusiastic "Ja". Jo has been learning German for the last two decades, hence she could get the gist of what he was saying, he wanted to have a picture with Jo! My wife does not like to be in the limelight, so I had to push her a little, and finally a picture was taken.

During the day we would walk into town and soak in the architecture, the atmosphere, we went to several concerts, visited on Sunday the Beautiful Cathedral for Mess (Austria is a catholic country). One day we booked the family Robinson trip with a local travel agent. In a minibus we were taken to where Maria and the colonel met, the house belonging to the family, the gazebo where they kissed for the first time and so on. I loved it because I love everything that is remotely connected to music and singing. On leaving us the driver made a remark "It is not true that the young postman betrayed the family as they were leaving for the US, as it is portrayed in the film". I think he wanted to tell us that not all Austrians had becoming fanatic Nazis, forgetting that the worse of them all was Austrian.

Bad Gastein.

The year after our son Marco who owned a flat in Bad Gastein, ski resort and SPA, invited us to spend some time with him. Marco, daughter-in-law Andrea, wife Jo, and granddaughters Monica and Daniela were already in Bad Gastein. I flew to Salzburg, went to the railway station and bought a ticket to Bad Gastein. To while the time away waiting for my train departure, I decided to walk about the city centre, looking for a suitable place where to have lunch. I saw an Italian restaurant and went in. The family who ran it where from Taranto like my mother, and its pictures decorated the walls. I asked the waitress what she recommended "Fresh fish ". "Fresh fish in Salzburg? I thought Austria was land locked! "The waitress replied "I have a friend in Venice who delivers freshly caught fish to the restaurant doorstep 2/3 times a week by car. It takes him three hours." I needed no more convincing and ordered fish and drank Pinot Grigio with it. Excellent. Back to the railway station I caught the train and after a couple of hours arrived in the centre of Bad Gastein, I could not believe that on one side of the railway station there were skiers skiing on a slope! I left the station and walked to my B&B perched on top of a hill. It was a pretty family run B&B built in typical Austrian style, plenty of wood everywhere, balconies graced with pots overflowing with geraniums and other flowers, spotlessly clean. I had to go to a B&B because there was no room at Marco's inn, their flat was in a block in the suburbs, about a mile and a half away. My room had a balcony facing the mountains, and every morning at about 0600 the sun would rise behind the mountains and in a few seconds illuminated the valley, it was like somebody switching on a gigantic light. Every morning I would not miss that spectacle. Sometimes my family would join me for breakfast, but every day I would walk to their flat to have lunch and dinner with them. The weather was very cold and dry, the temperature at night would go as low as -10c, but during the day the glorious sunshine raised to 0 or just above.

In order to go for walks I was wearing two pairs of trousers and socks, my British rambling boots, vest shirt, jumper and a duck down jacket. We went for walks in the woods nearby where we could have a hot drink and a slice of strudel in wooden huts. One day with a map in my hand I walked to the nearest town, about three miles, explored it, had a hot chocolate and walked back. All the fountains and waterfalls were frozen, and the ice had created icicles sculptures. My two granddaughters were still young enough to enjoy playing with grandad, we built snowmen, had snowballs fight in the sunshine. We went at Christmas time, and on Christmas day we went to church in the nearest one. On New Year eve Marco and Andrea did not want to wait for midnight in the town centre, but Monica wanted to go so she, Jo and I went, All the streets were crowded with revellers, all the bars and restaurants were open, the music was overflowing into the streets. At midnight fireworks started, it was magical.

Before leaving we went to the Spa, it consisted of a huge pool filled with very hot spring water, some of the pool was under cover, then you could go outside without cover, and the difference between the water about 30c warm and the outside temperature at about 2c was immediately felt, the trick was to keep as much of your body under water.

Soll.

Last year I went back to Austria, this time by coach with a small family owned company, Alan Philips. We stopped overnight in a hotel in Koln, then proceeded to our final destination, the hotel Tyrol in the town of Soll. The hotel was comfortable, the staff very friendly and helpful, the food delicious. Soll is a small town situated on the Austrian side of the Dolomites, at about 700 metres of altitude, to me it epitomizes the typical Austrian village, made mostly of wooden two storey buildings, the balconies full of flowers, with its inhabitants making a leaving out of tourism and farming.

Alan took his coach to the highest alpine pass in Europe, the Gross Glockner, altitude 3200 metres. He parked the coach and gave us an hour to satisfy our curiosity, take pictures and have a hot drink in the refuge. We were walking on tarmac but among a glacier. During the trips I noticed that the meadows were immaculately cut, then the grass was gathered in long strips, collected and taken away to feed the animals in winter. What was left were miles and miles of land that looked like a gigantic green carpet, without a weed or a blade of grass out of place. It was incredible. You could not see any litter on the ground, not even a spent match. One morning the hotel informed us that Soll municipal band dressed in Tyrolean costume would parade and play music, ending the parade in a small outdoors theatre around the corner from the hotel where a concert would follow free of charge. Of course, I and most of our party went to the theatre and we enjoyed a feast of music and singing.

On Sunday the same band paraded again, ending his playing outside Soll Catholic church. I believe all Soll population was there bar the sick, all in costume. I entered the church and the wardens divided us thus, females to left and males to the right. All churches I have been to in Austria are full of paintings, ornate golden ceilings and St. Anthony statues. One evening there was a festival in Soll, and the main street was illuminated, all bars and restaurants were open, and rivers of beer were flowing. In a corner a small group was playing the instrument that became famous in the film "The third man". Da dada da dadan…. I sat in the beer garden of a hotel and listened to Austrian music and yodelling.

The last day it was free, I went to reception and asked the pretty and welcoming receptionist what she suggested I went to see. She told me to take a bus or walk to a cable car station about a couple of miles at the back of the hotel and take a cable in order to get to the highest peak. I followed her instructions, and the cable car unloaded me half way, I took this break to sunbathe in half moon shaped wooden chairs. After a while and a beer, I walked to another cable car station and boarded a cable car heading to the summit. I noticed that quite a few hardy and very fit souls were walking to the summit. I left the cable car and I was overwhelmed from what I saw: around me at 360 degrees I could only see up to the horizon dozens of snow-capped mountains, nothing else. The sun was shining, and I inhaled the pure fresh air and felt near to God because only a superior being could have created such a beauty. My only regret was that nobody of my friends and family were there to share that beauty with me. I will never forget that view.

Killarney.

Jo's sister Mary had married Paddy in Killarney, a beautiful tourist town in Ireland. Killarney is surrounded by lakes and parks, the ideal place for walking. Paddy's house was on the main road between Killarney and the park, opposite to one of the park's gates, about a mile and a half from the centre. I like the Irish, I called them the Italians of northern Europe, because we have a lot in common: Religion, the love of singing, women, and in general some joie de vivre. Paddy introduced me to Poteen, a very strong drink that he made in his garage. I knew it was illegal, so I asked him if he ever had any trouble with the law "Oh no" he said in his Irish accent "The local Bobby is a friend of mine and he buys my poteen".

One day we had no water in the house, so Paddy and I went to inspect the pipe and found a leak. So, while we were waiting for the council to send someone to fix it, we wrapped a bicycle tyre around it, put stones around the leak, and covered it all with soil. The morning after two council workers rang the doorbell "Morning, will you show us where is the leak?" Paddy and I walked with them to the spot and showed them our handiwork. They put it all back, shook our hands and commented "Excellent work, we could not have done any better." Turned and started walking back to Killarney. Going to town with Paddy was an experience in itself, everybody knew him because his family owned a petrol station cum minimarket, and it was a non-stop of greetings, shaking hands or touching cap, accompanied by laughter. I could not tell a word of what they were saying but joined in the laughter all the same. Paddy had decided to go solo instead of working in the family business and had become a pest controller. Sometimes he took me on his work, and I leave it to your imagination what he told his poor clients, so that they believed he had done an excellent job.

We used to go to Killarney quite often, and one year I decided to hire a bike and explore Ireland on my own. I went as far as Tralee, I went on the ring of Kerry, a round trip full of beauty spots, tales of Queen Victoria stopping here and there, pubs and plenty of fresh air. At that time, I had taken up photography and I would park my bike and climb the mountains. Every 2/3 hundred yards I would stop and take a picture of the lakes, till I started walking down. In Killarney there was a pizzeria run by Italians, at lunch time I would buy a pizza and a beer and then carry on cycling.

Rome.

Every year I take some of my Italian language students to Rome and I give a guided tour of the Rome the Romans know and it is not in the guide books. For instance, I take them on the Aventine hill which I know very well because my Pio IX school was there, show them in my school and especially the chapel where we had to kneel on marble floors wearing short trousers. Then next door I point to the "Accademia nazionale di Balletto. I then head to the "Giardino degli aranci" or orange gardens where they can admire an amazing view of Rome while smelling the oranges. Next door to the garden there is the church of Santa Prisca dating to 450 AD. Next again there is the church of Sant Anselmo and moving on we arrive to "Piazza dei cavalieri di Malta" or The Knights of Malta square. In the square there are the headquarters of the knights, and whether by chance or intentionally the big keyhole in the main door is situated straight aiming to St. Peter's dome. If you place your eyes to the keyhole you see St. Peter. Till a couple of years ago all these places were almost deserted, but the BBC commissioned Alex Polizzi, the granddaughter of sir Charles Forte, to make a TV series about Italy, where her grandfather was born. Among other things she has taken

36

the cameras to nearly all the hidden beauty spot I knew, and now you have to queue if you want to see St. Peter through a keyhole.

Orvieto.

So, one year I decided to take my students to Orvieto. Orvieto is a medieval town built on top of a hill, it was used by the Popes as a fortress to stop invasions, since once the doors to the city are closed the town become impregnable. There was a problem, the assailants could wait till the town run out of water and then take her, the people of Orvieto understood that and built a very deep well "Il Pozzo di San Patrizio" or St Patrick's well which ended in a subterranean stream. The well has become a tourist attraction but you need strong legs and heart if you want to go down and up the 300 steps. Orvieto is also famous for its white wine and a magnificent Cathedral. But it is not famous for the sharpness of its police.

We were driving from Rome to Orvieto on the A1 or autostrada del sole, when I decided for a loo and drink stop at a motorway station. One of my students came to me to tell me that someone had taken from her bag all her money, cards and passport. I asked a waiter if he could help and he told me that those thefts were happening all the time on the A1. He gave me the number of the motorway police, I phoned, and I was told they were too busy with traffic problems and to report the theft to the nearest police station which happened to be in Orvieto. Once in Orvieto we headed to the police station when a policeman came out and asked, "Where are you going?" "We would like to report a theft." "But now is lunch time and my wife called me to say that the spaghetti is nearly cooked." "Can I report the theft to somebody else?" "No, we are all going to lunch at home, come back after 1500." We went to lunch as well and at 1500 we returned. We sat down and started explaining the theft when the policeman asked "I need the passport number" "But the passport has just being stolen…. that is one of the reasons we are here…." "I am sorry, but without the passport number I can't finish the theft report." In order to avoid being arrested for having treated a policeman without the due respect, I gritted my teeth, got up and thanked him for his help. We went back to our hotel in Ostia, a seaside resort near Rome. I used to live in Ostia and I knew that near the hotel there was a Carabinieri station. Carabinieri are the armed police who used to be the Italian Kings personal army, when the King decided to get rid of Mussolini he sent the Carabinieri to arrest him. The Carabinieri are the butt of many jokes because they are considered to be thick, and what about then the policeman in Orvieto? In the morning off we went to the Carabinieri station, where we were treated courteously by a captain who could also speak some English. The report was written without any reference to Passport numbers, and after ten minutes we were out in the sunshine blessing the Carabinieri for their expertise.

Germany.

Three years ago, I decided to try a train holiday. The holiday started from St. Pancras station in London. At the station I and other travellers were met by the holiday rep who would be with us till we returned home. We boarded a Eurostar train which at times would reach speeds comparable to the French TGV. The holiday was entitled "Rhine Valley Rail & River discovery. We stopped in the Rhineland capital Cologne, where we were left to discover the city. I visited the famous Cathedral and naturally bought some eau de Cologne for my wife Jo. Then we had a river cruise so that we could appreciate the beauty of the city from another viewing point. We carried on to our final destination, the town of Remagen and our hotel was the hotel Pilger, literally 200 yards from the railway station; the accommodation was for five nights B&B and dinner. The hotel was comfortable, clean and the staff very helpful. Remagen is famous for a terrible battle fought for keeping or destroying the Bridge. A film was made bearing the title "The bridge at Remagen." So, on day one I walked along the Rhine banks to find what was left of this bridge, and there is very little, a stump on either side of the Rhine. But its strategic importance must have been enormous because a large number of soldiers died on both sides. Then I went a walkabout to discover what Remagen had toto offer to the tourist. Remagen is a town of about 6000 inhabitants, and they have abdicated en masse their culinary prowess to the Italians; it does not take that long to walk its beautifully kept pedestrians only centre, but except for a few beer bars and a Restaurant with a German name, all other food outlets were owned by Italians, and were bearing Italian names. Austria is a Catholic country and Austria gave to Catholicism the last but one Pope, Ratzinger. I visited the beautiful Cathedral and a mini museum dedicated to Roman remains dug under and around the town. On day two we boarded a one-day cruiser for the journey though he UNESCO listed Rhine Gorge, beneath the famous Lorelei and past castles and picture books villages flanked by vineyards, then we travelled back by train. Day three featured a train journey on the narrow gauge Vulkan express through the Wooded Brohl Valley. We were told that the Vulkan express was functioning just that day for us, because May was still in the low tourist season, but even if it was May I was surprised how warm the weather was. We were also told the train would stop one station short of the end of the line main station. We enjoyed beautiful scenery, nibbles and drinks offered by the train steward, till we arrived at a station where the train stopped. The train would stop just for one hour, just to stretch our legs and explore the nearby village. I and a few more adventurous travellers left the train and started looking for the village, the road was narrow and very steep, so I made a mental note that I had to walk back to the train uphill. After ten minutes I looked back and realised I was the only one that still looking for the village, but as a rambler I did not give up. At last I found the village at the bottom of that road, but it was a farmer's village, there were no shops, cafes, public toilets, nothing.

I started walking back to the train, and suddenly "Die Banhof signs appeared, which even my non-existent German translated as "Railway station." I followed the signs, But I did not recognise the road I had come down from. So, I started ringing door bells, and the villagers opened their doors to a tired, thirsty Italian who could only articulate "Die Banhof?" And they gesticulated affirmatively, I was on the right tracks, even if by now the train would have left the station. Finally, I did find Die Banhof, only it was the main end of the tracks Banhof, and being low season was shut. The signs were correct, they indicated the main station. It was getting dark and I was in the middle of nowhere. Without mobile because on an escorted tour I thought not necessary to carry it. I had already walked only God knows how many miles, I was thirsty, hungry, tired and dirty, but I saw in the distance lights flickering, a sign of civilisation. Off I went to that direction and after one hour and a couple of miles more, I arrived in a farmer's village, this one inhabited by upper class people because the houses were large, modern and beautiful, but once again, no shops. So, I headed towards a house and rang the doorbell, and I did not know how to explain my predicament in German. A young man opened the door and quickly realised I had no German, so he switched to a passable English. H lets me in a fantastic house and asked me to sit down. He realised I needed refreshments and coffee and tea appeared together with Italian biscuits. He told me he was a part-time farmer and a part-time bank employee. He had two worries in his life, his only son at twenty years of age wanted to live as a hippy, sporting long hair, but having achieved no formal education, and not wanting to work as a farmer or in a bank. His other worry was **BREXIT**, yes you read it well, Brexit, and this before UK had formally initiated Brexit talks. I Thanked him for his kindness and explained that I had to return to the hotel Pilger in Remagen, was there a taxi service in the area? He picked up the Yellow Pages and looked for it, but apart from a chap who used to run with is car a taxi service to take children to school, there was nothing else. Then he suggested he took me to Remagen, not in his car because hi son was using it somewhere, but in his farm tractor. I had no alternative but to accept his offer. About more than an hour later I entered Remagen on a tractor, and my mind went to my Roman ancestors who returned to Rome after having conquered Gaul, Britannia, Spain and the rest of the known world, on horseback dragging under Arcs of Triumph chained slaves and looted treasure, and there I was on a tractor. SIC TRANSIT GLORIA MUNDI, they would say.

I was greeted by a sigh of relief from the rep who had in vain phoned my mobile. On the last day Mr. Pinger, who apart from the hotel owned a vineyard, organised a trip to his vineyard, we went on western style chariots, and he followed us on a bike. After having been dined and wined for free, the idea was that we would go to his cellar and buy some bottles of his wine. I, being born in Rome, was under the impression that good wines could be bought in Mediterranean countries where the strong sun would ripen the grapes just right for wine making. Once again I was wrong, because his Riesling white was superb, and I bought as many bottles as I could take back. In the evening Mr. Pinger had organised a farewell party, and the waitresses danced with the guests. In the morning while we were having breakfast, the plasma tv was showing us dancing. It has been one of my best holidays, apart from getting lost.

Madeira.

I have had a similar misadventure in Madeira. One day instead of walking back to my hotel I asked in my decent Portuguese which bus would take me there. I went on the bus, and the bus went more or less all over the island, stopping every few minutes. I did not have a clue as to when to alight, so I was straining my eye trying to recognise familiar features. After a couple of hours, the bus dropped me in the same spot where I had taken it, and another long walk was waiting for me. Madeira is a volcanic island belonging to Portugal, its location is such that the island enjoys a mild temperature all the year, the average is within 18 and 24c. The land is flat only for a few hundred yards by the sea, then it rises towards the summit of the volcano at 1200 metres, where the air is crisp and cool. I went on a spectacular funicular and on the top, there was a folk group from Peru called the Inti Illimani, playing their music dressed in their typical Peruvian clothes. They were at home because that eight was what they were used in Peru, I knew the group and their music, but I was still surprised to find them performing in Madeira. The massive interior of the volcanic cone is unexplored and was covered by a luscious semi-tropical forest. The flat land by the sea is dotted with cities like the capital Funchal, and villages, the airport, and a port where cruise ships land, so the people of Madeira over centuries have excavated the sides of the volcano and crated terrazzo mini farms, where since the volcanic soil is fertile they grow all sorts of crops. These farms are irrigated by "Llevadas" Our group was taken on a tour of a llevada, made of an irrigation channel excavated in the rock, next to the channel runs a path wide enough for only a person at the time to walk on, and on the other side were the small plots of land farmed by the locals. The views were amazing, but what was sad was that occasionally these plots were dotted by small wooden huts big enough for only one cow, and those animals were kept, milked and fed there, hardly ever going out. In the UK animal charities would have stopped that treatment immediately. We were taken to the llevadas by coach, and the female tour guide during the travel was explaining in Portuguese the history of the llevadas in an unbelievable singsong accent that she should have recorded and sold as a sleep tablet.

Madeira is also famous for a mad sleigh ride, not on snow but on the streets of Funchal. I was convinced by my friends to try it. The ride starts on a square situated on a hill, two persons at the time sit in the sleigh, driven at the back by a local. The sleigh is made of wood, and the brake is also made of wood. The driver starts pushing the sleigh on a narrow road going downhill and the sleigh starts going faster and faster, I thought the road was closed to traffic, but it was not, so we went at breakneck speed through traffic lights, crossroads etc. The brakes were never used, only to stop the sleigh at the end of the ride. I should have worn incontinence pants.

When on holiday I always look for local music or dance and one day I came across a leaflet advertising the "Madeira Mandolin Orchestra". The mandolin being a typical Italian instrument, I called a taxi and went to the theatre, the orchestra was made only of mandolins and played only Neapolitan music like "Funiculi' Funicula'. At the end of the concert the presenter told the audience that the orchestra would soon tour the UK. A year later I was looking at what the Lichfield Garrick theatre was going to show, and there it was, the "Madeira Mandolin Orchestra". Of course I went, and a good tenor was singing all the famous Neapolitan songs accompanied by the mandolins, it was very beautiful. Madeira is famous not only for the llevadas, but also for trying to help people to commit suicide on the streets of Funchal, or for the Madeira wine and cake, but above all for having given birth to Cristiano Ronaldo, one of the best footballers of the modern era. And that is why on one of the tours we were shown the ground where Ronaldo started kicking football, now the millionaire chap after a short time playing for Manchester United, plays for Real Madrid and Portugal, and now has moved to Juventus of Turin.

Chapter Four

Italian and British Behaviour Peculiarities

I do a lot of walking in order to (in vain) lose weight and keep fit. Sometimes I do it with a group, some other times on my own.

At the back of the flat where I live there is the disused rail track Walsall – Lichfield that Mr. Beeching axed in the 60's. It has been tarmacked to about two yards width and it is maintained by a charity called Sustrans. I collaborate with Sustrans by collecting rubbish and warning them when dead trees are blocking the path and similar circumstance when I need help. The track about three miles from my home narrows and becomes a dirt track, ending in a beauty spot with pools full of birds and swans. It is an ideal place for me to take exercise because the track starts only 100 yards from my home.

During my walks I am often met by fellow walkers or dog walkers, and often I am addressed by a complete stranger with this remark, 'Lovely weather today is not it? 'To which I am supposed to reply, 'Right you are, much better than yesterday,' then we part never to meet again. I find it odd, and if I greeted in Italy or anywhere else a stranger with a sentence like that I would be sent to a looney bin. The ever-changeable weather in Britain is the main topic of conversation, but I could be greeted by a stranger with a, 'Hi, how are you doing?' or not at all. I have been living in this country for 29 years but still find it odd.

Something even more odd is the normal greeting. When you go in a shop or a restaurant or even to a friend's house, before uttering, 'Good morning,' you have to check your watch and make sure it is before 1200 noon. I have been corrected hundreds of times for having said, 'Good morning,' at 1210, because I should have said, 'Good afternoon.' Only yesterday on the 14th of December 2017, I went to my local Argos store to buy a new electric razor. I greeted the cashier with a, 'Good morning,' and immediately he checked his watch and mumbled, 'Yes, it is only 1120.' Phew, I thought of being told off on the spot for using the wrong greeting. But what does it matter? He was more preoccupied that I greeted him correctly than taking care of my order. In the rest of Europe, we do use good morning and good afternoon, but we are not so meticulous. In Italy Buongiorno is used till there is daylight, or after 1200 noon one could say, 'Buon pomeriggio.' if he or she so wishes without being corrected. In the US, 'Have a good day,' is used with the meaning of all day long and so is, 'Buona giornata,' in Italy.

Another peculiarity of the British is queuing. If at a bus stop there are two people waiting, one is in front and one behind. They love it so much that they form queues even when it is not necessary. During one of my trips to Rome with my students, we were getting tired, and I suggested catching a taxi. Somebody suggested the bus; I strongly advised against it, but we waited for a bus. When our bus arrived, there was no orderly queue but a fight not to be left out. The doors closed, and we were jammed in without any space between one body and the other. My students were three ladies and of course we got separated. A few stops later the sheer push of more passengers getting on at every stop had pushed me against the front door. I was not ready to disembark but in order to let some passengers off I had to step off as well, and then get on again. When my three ladies saw me leave the bus they panicked and started calling me, and only relaxed when I got on again. After that nobody mentioned buses anymore.

As far as queuing is concerned I have become Anglicised and if in Italy I am queuing, and somebody tries to jump the queue (which it happens all the time) pretending that you are not there or with excuses like, 'I am collecting the pension of my great grandmother who is in hospital,' even shedding a tear for melodramatic effect, I sternly tell them to b off.

I had a shock about queuing many years when I flew from Rome to Heathrow. When I went to the transit check in desk in order to check in a flight from Heathrow to Birmingham, I completely ignored the queue. I was waving my ticket to the check-in personnel, but I was ignored while they carried on dealing with the passengers in the queue. I was not shouted at by people in the queue or by the personnel, I just did not exist. I felt like a stone-age man who had skipped a few thousand years of evolution. I got the message and went to the back of the queue. When my turn came I was checked in without any reference to my previous behaviour. A perfect lesson.

Another British behaviour peculiarity is to minimize the situation by using the sentence, 'It could be worse,' like a mantra. Twelve years ago, I had decided to buy the flat where I now live. I had booked a removal company to move my furniture to my new home. It was a terrible day weather-wise: hurricane force winds were nearly blowing people away, intermittent heavy rain was slashing the streets, but the removal company came and started packing and taking my belongings from a third floor flat to the parked van in the street without a reference to the weather. I was helping with carrying small items, when in the street I noticed that the wind nearly mowed down to the pavement the two people carrying a very heavy table. I approached them and said, 'It seems that I have chosen the wrong day for the removal.' But the company's boss smiled and replied, 'It could be a lot worse.'

How? A tsunami? An earthquake? A volcanic eruption?

There must be a genetic similarity in the behaviour of removal people everywhere, because let us go back to the day when I had sold my house in Rome and was ready to move for good to the UK. I had booked a local removal firm 'Scarozzi' to move my belongings from Rome to a lock up garage in Bloxwich, Walsall. As the departure date was getting nearer I became more and more anxious because Scarozzi did not seem to be preparing the relevant paperwork to get my belongings safely through customs in France and UK. At the time the UK was not an EU member and at Alitalia we moved from one country to another not only passengers but also cargo, so I was aware of the documentation needed. But every time I reminded Mr. Scarozzi, his unflappable mantra- like reply was, 'Non c'e' problema.' The equivalent of the British, 'No problem.'

The departure date arrived, the van was loaded, and I waved good bye to my belongings, may be for good. Scarozzi had all the odds stacked against him: no documentation, no other language spoken apart from Roman dialect, at the time sat-nav was still on the drawing board, and they had to deliver the goods to a lock up garage owned by an old lady who spoke only English. You can imagine my surprise when I received a phone call from Bloxwich telling me that Scarozzi had arrived and safely unloaded my furniture in her garage. From that day I have been teaching my Italian language students a very important phrase, 'Non c'e' problema.'

We Italians and for that matter the French and other jolly nationalities, are in the habit of hugging and kissing each other instead of shaking hands. I have tried to import this habit in the UK with varying degrees of success. One episode sticks to my mind; I had decided to take my British born and bred, Cambridge educated and classical music fan friend Tim, to a trip to charity shops in Mere Green, Birmingham. Within 150 yards there are six of them that I regularly patronise in order to buy books, language dictionaries, CD's for my music club, DVD's and the odd item of clothing. I would rather go on my own or with a male friend because if I go with my wife I end up doing all my shopping in thirty to forty minutes and then wait for her a couple of hours sipping coffees and reading newspapers in the Costa coffee bar. I remember once I texted her, 'I am in Costa,' and clicked the wrong button, and a reply came from my friend and student Diane, 'Which one, Costa Brava, Costa del Sol?' But this time Tim stuck by me till the last shop.

I had bought more stuff than usual, so I asked the lady at the till, 'I have already spent a lot today, could you give me a discount?'

She paused for a while then replied, 'We are a charity sir, and charities do not give discounts,' then looked at my hands full of items and added, 'Ok I will take a pound off this, 50p of that… and so on.'

When she had finished I told her, 'May I thank you the Italian way?' t

She replied, 'And what would that be?'

I added, 'With a kiss and a hug.'

She looked at me and paused, at that moment I realised that Tim was quietly leaving the premises, then she said, 'Come on then!'

I pulled her from behind the counter towards me, gave her a big kiss and a hug, then released her. I asked her, 'How was it?'

She replied, 'I'll tell you what, I feel better!' I said good bye and went out looking for Tim with a big smile on my face.

Before I found Tim, I encountered a stranger who started talking to me. His name was Pietro, a fellow countryman from Sicily. Later I will dedicate an entire chapter to him.

Sometimes the Brits can be interfering and nosey.

My son Marco is a councillor in Pelsall, Walsall, and at elections time I deliver his leaflets all over the village. One day I was driving back home having finished my work as a teacher, when I was flagged down by a traffic policeman, one of those who wear knee length boots and drive a motorbike. I stopped, looked at my watch and said, 'Good afternoon, I was not going too fast, was I?'

'No, someone has informed us that this car has been stolen.'

'But this car is mine!'

'Can you prove it?'

'Not now, but I have at home the V5.'

'May I see your driving licence?'

'No, I have not got it with me.'

'In that case you will have to take V5 and driving licence tomorrow to our police station.'

Next to him there was another uniformed policeman also on a motorbike, who had been quiet, but then he asked me, 'Do you have any ID on you?'

I showed him my Halesowen College ID, which had my picture and surname printed on it. He smiled at me and said in Italian, 'Where are you from? I am Sicilian.'

I said, 'Rome, but why was I stopped?'

'Because a nosey parker saw your car parked in a Pelsall street and since he did not recognise it as belonging to the area, reported it to us as stolen.'

'But I only park it there for a couple of hours at the time!'

He gave me back my ID, then talking to his colleague, 'Let him go, he is a friend of mine,' and he waved me off. This episode is part of several ones I label 'The Italian connection'.

It strikes me as odd the way the British behave in some circumstances. Once in a while I book a day trip with a Coach

Company called 'Majestic'. I like to book the Mystery tours because for £16 you get excellent value for money. On the day I turn up at The Clock in Bloxwich and at the correct time the coach arrives driven by Gordon who knows me because he used to drive coaches for the National Trust trips. Every time I book I beg him to find me a seat next to a gorgeous woman, but he never does. I remember a very unfortunate trip when he looked at his seating plan and told me where to sit. Moments later a huge woman sat by me. The poor lady's fat overlapped over me, nearly suffocating me. She was aware of her predicament and kept apologising, and I kept telling her I was ok.

Gordon, according to the weather situation, decides on the spot where is taking us. I do not remember where he took us that day, probably because my brain is still suffering from lack of oxygen. At one loo stop I spotted an empty seat at the far end of the coach and sat on it, but would you believe it, another very generously sized lady sat by me. This one was not aware of her enormous size, and since I could not avoid physical contact, she thought I was touching her inappropriately and complained to her husband, who started remonstrating with me. I tried to repress my laughter, got up and asked Gordon if I could sit on the guide chair by him. He was fully aware of my predicament (could it be because he caused it in the first place?) and let me.

But let us go to another mystery trip. Gordon decided to take us to Weston-super-Mare, where I had been a few times before. It is on the so-called British Riviera and on a sunny summer day is not a bad spot. But it was April and when we arrived we realised that the weather conditions were not ideal for a day to be spent on the British Riviera. We left the bus and we were left to our own devices to fill the time till 5 pm when Gordon was driving us back home. I started walking on the promenade towards the town centre, but the wind was very strong, I reckon up to gale force, thus pushing sand in my eyes, mouth and every other open receptacle in my body. But thinking that 'It could be worse,' the Brits were enjoying themselves. I shivered wearing warm clothes, wishing they were warmer, actually wishing I were not there at all, but they were all wearing sandals, shorts and a sun hat, after all they were on holiday! On the beach I saw parents pushing reluctant children on donkeys and families devouring sand decorated ice creams. So, thinking how my hero Bill Bryson would behaved in those circumstances and thinking that, 'IT COULD BE WORSE', I grabbed a sandwich and a beer and sought shelter from the gale in a park a couple of hundred yards from the promenade.

I was chatting to ladies who were taking their dogs for a walk and for bodily functions: it was very entertaining. But looking for something more diverting, I remembered that in coming to the park I had seen a sign for a theatre. What a stroke of genius, the theatre was showing a Ruth Rendell Mystery, which not only fitted with a Mystery tour, but would give me shelter till departure time. The cashier told me it had just started, which I did not mind. The excellent play ended just in time for me to catch the coach back home.

And now, 'La bella figura', an Italian National trait.

It can be translated by: you must look and dress at your best at any time of the day and night, whether at home or out, on holiday or at work, in a nutshell, always. I was born in La bella figura culture and I thought it was just normal to look your best all the time. In fact, we never think of it as our best, but just every day behaviour.

During one of my trips to the UK while I was engaged to Jo, she took me to Soho in London, thinking that because of the Italian influence on the area, I would feel at home. I was enjoying the day and the company, and since lunchtime was getting near, we went to a restaurant. While we were eating a man entered the restaurant, balancing a bottle on his head and wearing two red carnations on his ears. Nobody in the restaurant took any notice of him (British peculiarity, cool, calm and collected, one does not stare), the only person staring at him it was me. The man noticed that somebody was appreciating his 'Bella figura' and twirled a few times around our table, still balancing the bottle and not losing the two carnations, and after that he left the restaurant.

Some of the Ten British commandments are: thou shall not stare, thou shall not point, and so on. At the end of the meal I went to pay at the till, and before I opened my mouth the cashier told me, 'You are Italian, aren't you?'

'But how do you know?'

'When you entered the restaurant, I was sure you were Italian, possibly French. Look around the restaurant, you are the only person who at midweek lunchtime is wearing a blue suit, white shirt and matching tie.'

I looked around and he was right. But I was wearing what I rated as normal, not my Sunday best.

My brother-in-law Mario and my sister Gilda always took the art of Bella Figura to unprecedented heights. When living in the UK I would make trips to Rome and be their guest in their flat. In their bedroom there was a huge built-in wardrobe full of Mario's clothes only. Gilda's were in another wardrobe. From ceiling to floor there were rows of draws or hanging rails, each one full of white shirts, coloured shirts, short sleeve shirts, winter hat, summer hats, winter and summer socks, underpants, winter and summer trousers, V neck and polo neck jumpers, ties, jackets and suits, shoes, belts. Anything a gentleman could choose from. Since we were the same size, every time I went back to Rome he would give me some of his clothes, and I could tell some had never been worn before. So, every morning we would have breakfast, then it would take them a couple of hours to wash and dress. When they were ready, looking like they were going to a wedding reception or to a grand ball, I would ask where we were going and nine times out of ten they would reply, 'To the local market.'

We then started a passeggiata, I would translate it as a leisurely stroll, stopping for an aperitif and a mini cannolo alla siciliana, a Sicilian speciality, and off we went to the market, where they knew by first name every stall holder.

After having chatted and argued about the quality and price of the fish, bread, fruit, vegetables and everything else, they would pay and start another passeggiata back. I would usually be laden with the shopping. Once at home they would meticulously remove their clothes and put them in the relevant drawers and having put on pinnies they would start fitting (this is the correct word because if you opened their fridge you were faced by a wall of food, you could not put in a stamp) the food where possible, leaving out what was to be cooked.

During this process and after I would be admiring them from a comfortable chair like on G7 seat on the front row at the Grange theatre.

Mario had been a sailor in the navy during the war, then moved to the merchant navy and finally to a Ministry in Rome. Like all sailors he was an excellent cook, his speciality being fish. Gilda had learnt recipes from Grandma and mum and was equally good. Once the cooking was finished we sat and ate.

I must explain that a peculiarity of Italian families it is that to show how much they appreciate your company and friendship, they feed you like a turkey ready for Christmas, and the guest, in order to appreciate their hospitality, has to eat everything placed in his dish. They did not take no for an answer. Every time I was their guest I would be back three to four pounds heavier. I did try to minimise the intake, but after eating starters, two first courses (a soup and a pasta dish), a main course with several vegetables, fruit, and coffee, Gilda would try to feed me again.

'Antonio try a bit of this fresh buffalo mozzarella, it is a speciality you do not find in England.'

'But Gilda I have no more room.'

'Only a slice.' Or she would give me more vegetables.

'But Gilda I have no more room.'

'Come on it is only vegetables, they are good for you.'

My friend and student Louie was complaining to me that his sister behaved exactly like Gilda. I made a bet with him, he had to come to Rome and sample a normal every day lunch cooked by Gilda and Mario, and then compare it to his sister's. He accepted.

Louie is like me a football fan, so one Friday I rang him. 'Louie tomorrow morning I fly Ryanair from East Midlands airport to Rome. Come along and at lunch you will taste Gilda's cooking, and on Sunday we go to watch Rome playing at the Stadio Olimpico, back Sunday evening.' Louie accepted and on Saturday morning we met at East midlands airport. We had lunch at my sister's home, and Gilda won hands down. When we left the flat Louie could hardly breathe and conceded defeat.

The British as a race are reserved and shy, but when exceptions occur they are the epitome of eccentricity and extravagance. One example is Colin Such, vicar of St. Michael church, Leigh Road, Walsall. St Michael is situated a few hundred yards from the house where I used to live before and from the flat where I live now. Soon after moving from Rome I went for a walk and stumbled upon this medieval church. I went in and a Mess was on, I stayed and since the congregation was chanting "I believe in one Catholic and apostolic church...." I was sure to be in a Catholic church, also because Anglican churches do not have images and statues of saints, and this one did. The walls around and above the altar were decorated by pre -Raphaelite frescoes of angels and saints. I went home and told my staunch Catholic wife about my discovery, but she told me that St. Michael was not a Catholic church and therefore I had not absolved my Sunday Mess obligation. I replied that during my three years in a Catholic school, I and the other boys had to go to doctrine every week, and distinctly remembered that the priest told us that God knows our intentions, and since I was sure to be in a Catholic church I had absolved my obligation. She carried on with other fine points of doctrine like "Transubstantiation" whereby only the hosts and wine benedicted by a Catholic priest became the body and blood of Christ. I replied that St. Michael and all the churches that old had been Catholic churches until Henry VIII invented the Anglican church because the Pope would not grant him a divorce. The British population left Catholicism for the whim of a man, and had Henry VIII not existed, all churches would be still Catholic and all the UK population would still be Catholic. Anyway, there is only one God and it is the same God worshipped in all Christian Churches in the world, whether Catholic, Anglican, Presbyterian, Orthodox and so on.

When years ago I was a serious rambler, if the ramble was on a Sunday and I would see the spire of a church, I left the ramblers and went into the church, not minding at all whether it was Catholic or not. And in spite of muddy boots I was always welcomed and given a guided tour by the locals, proud to show their church to a visitor. Years ago, Jeff, a member of the congregation, asked me if I wanted to become an altar server. Since I had offered my services to St. Mary the Mount RC Church but I was not accepted, I said yes. On a Sunday if I am not on the rota as a server I go to St. Mary the Mount. After a short induction I started serving on a rota basis, on average twice a month. The rumour goes that I became an altar server only because at the end of the service the altar servers have to drink the blood of Christ to the last drop and eat the body of Christ to the last crumb, and somehow, I always manage to drink the blood of Christ. The rumour is of course unfounded. Colin became a vicar as a late vocation, that is he had a career as a solicitor before he was called by God to become a minister. Usually most men go to a seminary at eighteen and leave a few years later becoming priests without having had any experience of the world outside the seminary. Colin takes his flock to a pilgrimage every second year, but his preferred pilgrimages are to Italy. Having realised that not only I was Italian, but I also was a trained teacher, he started having Italian language lessons. I do not teach only the grammar, but I make my lessons more interesting by teaching the art, the culture and the music of my country. I told all my students to read the book "La bella lingua", by an American lady in love with the Italian language. In her quest to become perfectly fluent, she ended up at the "Dante Alighieri School" in Florence. In the last pages of her book she asked the Italian language teacher what else she could do to improve her Italian and the teacher replied "Watch films in Italian with either

Italian or English subtitles, and if even that fails, go to bed with the teacher." Even before I read that book I had started giving my students Italian films to watch at home, and as far as the other suggestion goes, I have hinted to it to my predominantly female students, so far with no success.

Two years ago, I joined the church pilgrimage to Italy. Our base was an hotel in Padua, opposite the Cathedral of St. Anthony, where I had never been even if he is my patron saint. I became their translator and facilitator. One day I suggested a trip to Venice, and I took them to the railway station. When in Venice the party split up, some, including Colin, his brother-in-law and his friend Amanda stayed with me. On foot I took them to all the main places in Venice, including the Florian bar in St. Mark square, where we listened to an orchestra while sipping coffees and heard tales of Casanova wooing his lovers somewhere in the Florian. Then I took them to the hotel Cipriani, the most expensive in Venice and one of the most expensive in Europe. We had a look in the magnificent marble interior till we reached a sign saying that only gusts could go further. Amanda wanted to go on a gondola, so I hired one and she graciously paid the bill. It was getting towards lunch time, so I asked the gondolier where they went for lunch and following his instructions we found a fabulous trattoria full of locals eating good food at a decent price. We carried on to the bridge of Sighs and the Rialto bridge, then we went back to the station and Padua. Colin and the rest of his party realised how important it is to understand the Italian language because when we went to see the" Cappella degli

Scrovegni", second in importance only to the Sistine Chapel for frescoes, mainly by Giotto and Cimabue. The only guide inside could only speak Italian and in a place visited by tourists from all over the world he should have spoken at least English.

From Padua we boarded a coach that took us on the A14 to Assisi, our next base camp. It was a long five hours trip; we arrived in Assisi at dusk and we were pleasantly surprised to find that our hotel "Casa del Pellegrino" was situated in the pedestrian centre of the medieval city. Colin said Mess in St. Francis of Assisi Cathedral, I bought a beautifully decorated print of "Il cantico delle creature", written by St. Francis to thank God for brother Sun, sister Moon and all living animals.

One day the "Giro d'Italia" or cycling tour of Italy was passing Assisi. I had always wanted to see the Cyclists at close range, so I went to a bend in the road where they would slow down and watched them passing by for an hour. Alas all good things come to an end and in the morning, we were driven to Perugia airport. Perugia is a fantastic city, capital of Umbria region which is advertised as "Il cuore verde dell'Italia", or the green heart of Italy. The tiny airport was only recently open to civilian flights, it only has two flights a day, one to Stanstead and one to Germany. In Stanstead we were collected by a coach and driven to Walsall. In Walsall a few days after our arrival Colin organised a party to celebrate our return. Italian 60's music was played and I started singing, then Italian food and wine arrived. Then Colin surprised us all by changing into a pantomime lady, wearing a blonde wig and a beautiful dress.

Apparently before having the call he had been a member of an amateur drama society. I then realised that Colin's love of everything Italian was great and the "Pilgrimages" apart from going to holy shrines, were also meant as an opportunity to bask in the sunshine and enjoy the food and the culture. In September 2018 we will be going to Sicily, I have noticed that one day we will visit the town of Marsala, famous for his dessert wine and I asked (jokingly) Colin why we could not use that wine during Mess, but the altar wine was bought by the Lichfield Dioceses and we have to stick to it.

Writing about eccentricities I must now mention my Djallabia. It is the everyday garment used in the hot middle east countries, it is one piece of cotton, in short it is what Lawrence of Arabia was wearing during the Arab revolt. I have bought it many years ago in a souk in Tunisia. The Arabs are famous for haggling, but the Italians are not bad either, so after haggling for half an hour in Italian, French and Arabic, the price went down to what I considered to be a fair price to both vendor and client. I started wearing it immediately because in a hot country it is the best garment to keep cool. I was complimented by other Arabs on how beautiful my Djallabia was. Back in the UK I had put it in a wardrobe and forgot about it. Occasionally in this country there is a heat wave when the temperature can reach 30c plus (in Rome it reaches 40c plus). On such a summer day I decided to wear my Djallabia. It was Sunday and I started wearing it in a clothes superstore called "Boundary Mills". All went well when I was approached by a true Arab who started chatting to me in Arabic. I uttered the few words I know in Arabic and went to the exit.

Next, I had to go to Wolverhampton railway station to pick up my wife Jo returning from a visit to our daughter Laura, who at the time was living in Manchester. Jo was looking for her husband, not for Lawrence of Arabia, when she realised how I was dressed said "I am not coming with you dressed like that!" To which I replied "Fine, you know where the taxi rank is." And started walking towards the exit. She started following me three paces behind, like Prince Philip walks behind the Queen. Suddenly a beautiful black woman wearing a Djallabia walks towards me and when our eyes met she said "Beautiful Djallabia sir" and I complimented her by saying "Not as beautiful as yours." Then I turned to Jo and gesticulated, you see somebody appreciates the way I dress. Later on, I had to go to Mess, and as usual I walked to St. Michael. I sat down pretending I was dressed normally, but I could feel all the gazes aiming to my direction. After Mess we have a cup of tea and biscuits in the church hall and socialise for a while. After a bit my friend Jeff came to me and told me I looked like the singer Demis Roussos, then one of the choir ladies asked me what I was wearing under it. I replied "The same as what the Scots wear under the kilt." On leaving the church I was greeted by the female vicar Sue. We shook hands and I told her "Sue I apologise for coming to church dressed like this." To which she replied "Not at all Antonio, you look fine, I wished I could wear one layer only on a hot day like today." What I do not understand is why when I wear a long dress when I serve on the altar nobody finds it odd, but if I wear a similar dress, only a different colour, people think it is strange.

My father-in-law Wilf owned a holiday house in the Snowdonia area in Wales. We used to go to spend may week-ends and holidays in Wales. Wales is on of the rainiest regions in the UK, but in 1976 a very hot summer happened. My family and the Clarke family, about 20 of us, were spending a few days in Wales. The land around the property was farmed mainly for cattle and sheep grazing. That summer all the ponds and streams were the animals drank dried up, and the cows knew there was water in the house, so they came to the house mooing loudly, we gave them buckets of water, but the farmer told us not to, because a cow needs to drink many gallons of water and moisture from the grass, and a bucketful would only prolong their agony. Years later we were in Wales again, and I went to visit Portmerion, an Italianate seaside village built by the usual eccentric British landed gentry, who was in love with Portofino and tried to build another Portofino in Wales. Portmerion has become a tourist attraction and you have to pay to enter it. It has developed an industry of distinctive Portmerion ceramic, and also thrives on tourism. The village is made of hotels, restaurants, museums, and some houses. In the centre there is a square with a statue in the middle of it. I went to read the inscription at the base of the statue, and I could not believe my eyes when I read **"TO THE GLORIOUS SUMMER OF 1976"**. Only the British would erect a statue to a summer!!

Chapter five

Italian Bureaucracy versus British

One of the many reasons that made me decide to resign my job with Alitalia and start afresh in the UK was the incredibly inefficient Italian bureaucracy, sometimes inefficient to the point of becoming ridiculous. Italy is a G7 member, and yet I can only describe its bureaucracy as third world. I must start when I was still working at the airport and I needed to renew my passport, which was used for leisure and often for work. At the airport I made the acquaintance with a retired policeman, who supplemented his pension by helping passengers to solve problems on the spot. He would come to the airport with his briefcase, often meeting old clients or intervening to help new ones. In Italy the passport is released and renewed by the police, and I had applied for renewal to the relevant office. I waited three or four months, then I started to enquire over the phone with no success. So, one day I decided to investigate in person, and after having waited the customary couple of hours I was received in the office where my passport was held up. I introduced myself and asked why my passport was taking so long to be renewed; the person in charge showed me two passports, both bearing the name Antonio Longhi, only the other Antonio Longhi had a criminal record. However, his picture and mine bore no resemblance, we were born in different cities in different years from different parents. I asked what was the problem and I was told they were still investigating the matter.

When I went back to work I asked the retired policeman if he could help. He picked up a phone, had a short conversation, then told me, 'Tomorrow go to the same office and you will get your renewed passport.' I did and unbelievingly all the problems of having the same name and surname of a criminal had been solved overnight, and on leaving I received a military salute.

I had already been living and working in the UK for several years when I received a phone call from my mother, who was very agitated. Before leaving for good I had cancelled my residence in Rome and elected my Mother's address as 'domicile', that is the address where I could still be contacted in Italy. She had received a letter from the tax office stating that they believed that when I had sold my villa at Infernetto, in the suburbs of Rome, I had avoided paying the correct tax amount by declaring to have sold it at about 30 % less than the average for a similar house in Infernetto. On such and such day and date there was going to be a court case and I was invited to elect a solicitor for my defence. I told my mum to relax, and that I would take care of it. The prosecutor had to prove his point and as far as I knew he had no evidence. I did not elect a solicitor to represent me. The trial day arrives and goes and a few weeks later my mother forwards me a letter from the tax office: I had been tried in absentia and I was found innocent for lack of evidence. Just think of the money the Italian Government had wasted in trying to convict me while that money could have been spent to improve the IQ of some people working in the passport department. But in Italy a citizen is guilty unless proven innocent.

An Italian male knows that he can be sure of two things: of doing his military service and of dying; so far, I have escaped both predictions. When I was nearing my 18th birthday and I was in my last year of secondary education, planning to go to University, I received the green card telling me to go to Via Della Greca for a physical examination. If I passed it I would have been enrolled for 18 months of military service. I knew that I was going to receive the green card, and I had enrolled the help of my brother-in-law Mario, who by then had become a bureaucrat in the ministry of transport and therefore knew how to deal with bureaucracy. He found out that because I was the only male in my household and my mother was a widow, I could be exempted on the grounds that as the only male I was the bread winner. Nothing was further from the truth, I was a full-time student and my mother was the bread winner, because after my father's death she had started a small business. Mario and I spent several days going to the various offices involved in giving me an exemption certificate from the military service, and we succeeded. On the day of my physical examination I left school and went to Via Della Greca, when my turn came I had to strip naked and had to endure all sort of tests, and I mean all. At the end I got dressed and the military doctor told me, 'Bravo, abile e arruolato,' Well done, you have an able body therefore you are enrolled. At that point I produced my exemption certificate, he had a look and filed it in my

69

folder. I asked if I could go back to school, but he asked me to stay and help him in his job.

'You see you are one the few educated teenagers here today, you could help me with typing reports. I agree that for somebody like you military service is a waste of time, but for the majority it is a way to improve their chances of leading a normal life, we give them an education, we train them in a trade and when they go back home they are ready to face the challenges of life.'

My father-in-law Wilfred had bought a couple of properties in the Snowdonia Park area, and we would spend many week-ends there. Since I had married his daughter I was a member of the party, and would do a lot of driving, but still I was not confident with driving on the wrong side of the road, so I always made a mental note to park in the direction I was going to resume driving. One day we were going shopping in the Post office-cum-newsagent cum-grocery store in Maentw-u-wrog (Welsh speaking readers forgive my spelling). I should have parked on the left side of the road but could not because there was a rock cliff and no parking space, so I parked in the P.O. car park on the right side. Having done the shopping, I, mother-in-law Ena and wife Jo, got in the car. I switched the engine on and merrily started driving on the right side of the road because that is where I had parked the car. That road is full of bends and I could not gather speed. At a bend I saw another car driving in my direction on the same side of the road. I could not avoid the collision because if I swerved to the right I was going to end in the river Madoc, if swerved to the left I would hit the rock behind which the other car had emerged. So, I braced myself for the head on collision. We were not hurt badly only because both cars were going slowly.

I passed out and woke up in the Cottage Hospital in Blaenau. I had injuries to my head, and knees, and was in a pleasant room. A nurse offered me a cup of tea and asked if I was ready to receive a policeman in order to give a statement. By the way I was treated I thought I was in a B&B. I agreed to see the policeman and gave my evidence; what else could I say apart from that I had momentarily forgotten I was driving in the UK? Having performed my duty with the law, I was asked to meet with my family in a community room. Ena had a jaw injury and Jo several scars over her body. The car was a write off. But what a difference to what would have happened had the accident occurred in Italy! We were offered sandwiches and drinks because it was lunch time, then the doctor who had looked after us asked to see me. I went into his private study and he told me his tale.

During the war he had fought in Italy, and in Naples he had fallen in love with a Neapolitan woman. They got married in the British Embassy in Naples, that means on British soil, and never registered their marriage with the Italian government. The war ended, and he and his bride came to live in the UK, where he started a career as a GP. Between the end of the war and the time I met him thirty years later, he had fathered a boy and moved many times because of his job, ending in Blaenau in the middle of the Welsh mountains. But the implacable Italian bureaucracy had followed his movements and on the day his son turned 18 two carabinieri in uniform knocked on his door in Blaenau asking to deport his son to Italy where he was going to do his military service, and if he refused he could be sent to jail. The doctor explained that his son was a British national, and his only relationship with Italy was that he had an Italian mother. At the end of a long argument the Carabinieri went back empty handed.

It is very hard to believe how the Italian military service office came to know of the tenuous relationship between this boy and Italian citizenship, how for 18 years they had followed the movements of this family. If Italian bureaucracy could be so efficient all the time we could easily become the leading nation of the G7.

I do criticise my country a lot, but at the same time I defend her when other people criticise her because I feel 100 % Italian.

After arriving in the UK at 48 years of age I tried to go back to the travel business, but at that age every time I went for an interview I was told I had all the qualifications and experience, but the panel implied I was too old. Bear in mind that when I came to the UK I was at the peak of my mental and physical condition, I was a stone and a half lighter, and I was running five miles three times a week. The only profession that did not mind my age was teaching, so I became a teacher. When I was 66 years old the last school where I was teaching, Queen Mary's Grammar in Walsall, decided for budget reason they had to dispense with my services. I was pensioned off. Within a few weeks I received a British pension, and since when I could not find a position within the travel industry I was doing odd jobs or voluntary work, for about a year I had paid voluntary contributions toward my future pension, and they had been included in calculating my British pension. Having finished with my British pension I dedicated my time to getting an Italian one.

Enter Mrs. Maura Barr, working at the Italian Consulate in Birmingham as Patronato ACLI adviser. ACLI stands for Associazione Cattolica Lavoratori Italiani. All Italian Trade Unions and Religious associations having realised that workers having once finished their working life had to negotiate their pensions with that monster called bureaucracy, had created 'Patronato' associations in order to help them with pensions and other problems. Mrs. Barr is a shining example of somebody working very hard to beat that monster. She is a Milanese and works to a Milanese work ethic; she is very knowledgeable, and willing to help. If more people like Mrs Barr worked for the Italian bureaucracy, things would be much better. I went to her so that she could give me the facts of how, when and how may N.I. contributions I needed in order to obtain an Italian pension. I had kept all the paperwork given to me when I resigned from Alitalia, and we calculated together that I was within the age group which at the time was 57 years, and that I was short of a number of contributions. She also told me that in order to reach that number I could use 'figuratively' the N.I. I had obtained in this country working as teacher. Figuratively meant that according to EU law any worker working in any EU country could add the N.I. earned working in a country different from the one where he was born, in order to reach the minimum required for his pension in his birthplace. They would be added as number, but would not increase the amount to be paid, because they could only be used once for that purpose, and I had already used them for my British pension. Mrs. Barr, once she had given me the information I needed, left me to carry on by myself, because she knew I was computer literate, while she needed to help the other Italians working in the Midlands who could not complete their task by themselves.

I sent the relevant documentation to the INPS office in Rome, INPS was the state pension pot where I had paid my contributions while I was working in Italy, and I explained in a covering letter that if they 'figuratively' added the British ones, I would reach the required number.

INPS came back to me saying that I did not qualify because INPS (and the Italian government) did not recognise as valid the year of voluntary N.I. I had paid when I could not find a job. I go on the Internet and find EU resolution xyzps approved in year blabla, that states, 'Every N.I. contribution obtained in any EU nation and recognised as valid in any EU nation must be considered valid in any other EU country.' My voluntary contributions had been recognised as valid by the British Government and included in my British pension calculations, therefore had to be recognised in Italy too because the EU law is stronger and supersedes any Italian law. And with this argument I go back to INPS, but I was smashing my head against a brick wall. So, I contacted my MEP (Member of European Parliament) Liz Lynn and asked her help in order to fight my corner. She said she will do her best, and that the EU was already on my side since they had voted that resolution. She gave me the name of an EU bureaucrat who would follow my case in Brussels. I started to phone him or email him at regular intervals, but all I got was sympathy.

One day he finally told me the truth, 'Mister Longhi, unless we, the EU, declare war to the Berlusconi Government you will never get your pension, because you have opened a can of worms, and if you win your case, the Italian government will be deluged with request like yours or similar. You are the first person who has challenged the Italian government using an EU resolution, and if they accept defeat your case will become a test case.'

That answer filled me with pride, but it did not help me. The only solution was to go back to work and earn more N.I. Having done that, I recalculated my N.I. excluding the voluntary ones, and I was over the minimum by about a dozen. That will do, I thought, and immediately I requested an updated N.I. table to Newcastle (where the relevant office is situated) so that I could apply again to INPS for my pension. I received the documentation, but I noticed that if I added the N.I. in that document to the Italian ones, I was under the minimum by about twenty. I was sure that Newcastle had made a mistake, so I phoned, and a very nice lady answered me. I explained my problem and she replied, 'Mister Longhi when you started residing in this country for good, the English Government gave you 20 N.I. contributions as a welcome gift, unfortunately those are not valid forever, and I had to take them off recently.' I was speechless for a long time, and she asked me what was wrong, and when I had explained she said, 'Mister Longhi I will personally add another 20 N.I. to your total and send you an updated table. Enjoy a long and happy retirement!'

And so, I started living on two pensions plus the occasional private lesson. When I was working, HRMC used to have an office open to the public in Midland Road, Walsall. It was very useful because sometimes I went to compile my tax return there, and because of the nature of my work, I could have between six and nine P60's (for the non-British readers a P60 is a document given by employers to every worker, stating how much tax had been paid and how many National Insurance contributions had been paid during that year.) But I and my usual adviser in about 30 minutes would sort it out. Also, as a pensioner I was required to fill in a tax return which I did on my own. At the time my Italian pension was taxed in Italy, even if INPS knew I was living in the UK, and when I compiled the tax return, in the blank page I always put a note: do not tax me again on my Italian pension because I have been already taxed at source.

Everything went smoothly when one day I received a letter from a Mr. Joshi, tax inspector. In it he informed me that I should have paid tax on my Italian pension in the UK, since I was a UK resident and used Hospitals, roads, trains and everything necessary to lead a normal life, in the UK. He also mentioned the relevant EU law. I replied that I did not ask INPS to be taxed in Italy, that INPS were aware I was leaving permanently in the UK and that on top of it they should have been aware of the relevant EU law. I should not be considered a tax dodger because I had paid tax, only I was not aware that I was taxed in the wrong country. And INPS and HRMC should have been aware and corrected the situation from day one, because every year I had explained in the tax return blank page my situation.

Since I had done nothing wrong I asked Mr. Joshi to get in touch with INPS and ask for all tax paid in Italy to be transferred to UK. Mr. Joshi refused and asked me to do it. At that point I went to Mrs. Barr for help. She explained that she had had to work on similar cases in the past, and it takes about a year to get the money from Italy to the UK. I told Mrs Barr that I had explained to Mr. Joshi that while he was demanding from me documentation and payment within weeks, in Italy it would take months, maybe years.

Mr. Joshi had demanded that I pay immediately from my savings the tax that had been paid in Italy, at the same time requesting INPS to refund me that tax. I pointed out that what he was asking was illegal, because until, if, and when I would get that money back, I was paying tax in two EU countries. Mrs Barr suggested that first of all we asked INPS to pay my pension intact, at the same time pay Mr. Joshi, and ask 'Agenzia delle Entrate' literally Agency for money coming in, to refund me. I felt cheated by this arrangement, so I wrote a letter to Mr. Joshi complaining about this very unfair arrangement because I would be out of pocket for a considerable amount of time. I also mentioned that since HRMC could not force big corporations like Amazon, Starbucks, Google and many more to pay taxes in the UK instead of using tax avoidance schemes, the tax inspectors were trying to get some few thousand pounds from people like me, just to show that they were working. And since it was near Christmas I finished the letter with an ironic Merry Christmas to him and his family, fully aware that he was a Muslim. I was expecting a reply of some sort, but it never came.

My Odyssey to get back 6000 euros that 'Agenzia delle Entrate' now owed me lasted three years. Three years spent sending emails, faxes, making phone calls etc. These are the main points. After about six months Mr. Spinetti, who was in charge of my case, asked me the date of my inscription to AIRE or Associazione Italiani Residenti Estero, Association of Italians resident abroad. When I went to the Registry Office in Rome to cancel the Longhi family as residents in Rome, nobody warned me about AIRE. Anyway, I did subscribe because I heard about it by chance, during a visit to the Italian Vice Consulate in Birmingham. Of course, I could not remember the exact date. Mr. Spinetti then asked that date to the registry office in Rome (which serves about two million residents) and naturally months went by and he did not get any answer. One day I had decided to solve the problem, sent an email to the AIRE office within the Italian Embassy in London and got an answer within twenty minutes. I still remember the wording, 'Kind and dear fellow Italian, you became a member of AIRE on XYWZ 2002. I hope this information will speed up your refund request.' I immediately forwarded that information to Mr. Spinetti. I was in fact doing his work!

More months went by and at last I got a letter from Agenzia delle Entrate informing me that my request had been accepted and was up for payment asap. In the era of on-line banking, I expected to be paid within a week at most, so after a week I contacted Mr. Spinetti again. He had forgotten to tell me that my folder had been transferred to the BANK OF ITALY in Rome, and I would be paid by them asap. Can you imagine The Bank of England doing a similar job?

I realised then why Agenzia delle Entrate was called so, because it worked only for money coming in, not for money going out, otherwise it should have been called Agenzia delle Entrate e Uscite, uscite meaning going out. Now I only had to tackle the Bank of Italy in Rome, I was on familiar grounds. I phoned them to ask for news, using my best Roman accent. The guy in Rome was not impressed, but after prodding him for an answer he replied, 'Prima di Natale,' before Christmas. At the time we were in November. I could not believe my eyes when a cheque for six thousand Euros arrived a few days before Christmas.

Chapter Six

Suing

I do not complain or sue unless I am 100 % convinced I am right. Over the years I have acquired a good knowledge of complaining with different methods according to the matter at hand: with corporations using the Ombudsman, with individuals or small businesses using the small claims court, and occasionally with irony and wit. So far, I have always won, to the point that my son Marco, the Walsall councillor and now Mayor of Walsall begs me, 'Dad please do not sue the Council, I am known there'

Twelve years ago, I was living in a top of the range flat on the third floor in Streets Corner, Walsall. I was only the second person to rent the flat. When winter arrived, I switched the central heating on and noticed that the boiler situated in the kitchen was leaking. I phoned the letting agent and had no joy, so I phoned the office of the builder and owner of the block of flats. The answer I got was, 'Strange, nobody has complained before.'

'I do not care whether I am the first or the last, I am asking you to fix the boiler.'

As a race the British do not like to complain. During meals I have heard people at my table complain about the poor quality of the food they were eating, but when the waiter comes and asks, 'Was everything ok?'

The general consensus reply is, 'Excellent meal thanks.'

I come from another culture and if I pay for a service or buy something, and something goes wrong, I complain and expect to be refunded. Since even my call to the owner of the flat did not produce the effect I expected, I called Walsall Town Hall, where there is a Landlord Tenant Relations Officer. I forget now the proper title.

The morning after a young man comes from the Town Hall, and on inspection finds out that the leak comes from the roof, and when it rains, the rain finds its way down to the gas boiler. He told me it was a serious hazard and the boiler may even explode.

'I am issuing the owner with a repair order to be made immediately, and if he does not comply I will force him to rehouse you in another flat for free till the repair has been carried out.' The morning after scaffolds were erected and roofers were repairing the leak. This is what it means to live in a civilised country.

When I arrived to the flat I noticed that there was a phone, but the phone had been disconnected by the previous tenant. I called BT from my mobile and asked for the line to be reconnected.

'We will send an engineer within a week.'

'But asap please because I am using my mobile which is more expensive. By the way how much I am expected to pay?'

'It depends on how long the engineer will take.'

Two weeks went by before the engineer arrived. He went down in the street where the box with all the cables was located. I could see him from my window, it took him thirty seconds to reconnect my line. He came up, tested the phone and was collecting his tool box when I asked, 'How much should I pay for your work?'

'Nothing at all. Good bye.'

When the first bill arrived, I was charged about £150 for the engineer's work. I did not pay it and started a tug of war with BT. They did not believe the engineer told me there was no charge, but I replied that not even a brain surgeon charges £150 for thirty seconds, and not only I was not going to pay, but expected BT to foot my mobile bill, because it had taken them two weeks to send someone for thirty seconds work; during those two weeks I had to use my mobile all the time.

Time went on between a payment request and a refusal, till I bought the flat where I live now. There I was faced with the same problem, there was a deactivated phone line, and like in the other flat I could see the box. I thought that if I entered in another contract with BT using my name, immediately they would start trying to get £150 from me or refuse to reconnect me. I had to ask reconnection to BT because they had laid down and owned all the telephone lines, but once reconnected I could move on to a cheaper provider. I called BT and told them that I had just bought the flat and wanted to be reconnected.

'And what is your name, Sir?'

'Peter Ustinov.'

Notwithstanding my thick Italian accent, I was reconnected. Then till I managed to move to another provider, every time BT phoned and asked to speak to Peter Ustinov, I replied, 'Speaking.'

I was happily living in my new home when I decided to buy a Blackberry mobile. This move implied leaving O2 which had been my provider for years and move to Three; with O2 I was on a pay as you go contract while with Three I had to pay a monthly fee.

Everything went smoothly for a few months, when suddenly I could not receive or make calls and texts.

I phoned Three technical support and I was told to go through motions I had already tried with no success.

At the end of the conversation the technical support asked, 'Have you tried to make a call from Aldridge (4 miles away) and see if the phone works from there?'

'But I want my mobile to work everywhere and not just from Manchester or Aldridge. Until I was with O2 my mobile had always worked for years, now is dead.'

I was told to take my mobile to the Three shop in the centre of town. After the usual pleasantries they performed the usual checks I had already done at home over the phone, and they came up with a brilliant solution.

'Your phone is dead, buy a new one!'

'But this one is only a few months old.'

Anyway, I was convinced to buy another phone, which worked in the shop, but stopped working the moment I was at home. I went back in town and asked Three for a refund.

'We do not give refunds, we can exchange it for another phone.'

I left the Three shop and went in the O2 shop thirty yards away, bought a phone, went home and it worked perfectly. I put in writing my grievances to the Three customer service, asking for a refund for the phone I bought and would not work, but naturally they refused. I immediately stopped the direct debit I had set up to pay the monthly fee, went to a second-hand shop and sold the dud Three phone. I got some money back. Then Three started bombarding me with request to pay my monthly fee, so I referred the matter to the communications Ombudsman who adjudicated in my favour. I sent a copy of the Ombudsman decision to Three customer service, and their response was to send me a threatening letter stating that if I did not pay my monthly fee again they would send the bailiffs.

I had reached the point when I was past caring and ignored the threat. A bailiff letter arrived it and I ignored it as well. Then one day I received a phone call.

'This is Three debt recovery office; may I speak with Mister Longhi?'

'I am afraid not, I am his butler. Mr. Longhi in order to avoid unreasonable money requests, bailiff's letters and phone calls from Three, has emigrated to Australia, and I am not at liberty to give you his forwarding address. Good day sir.'

Nevertheless, three carried on trying to contact me again several times, till about twelve months after I went to their shop, they gave up.

About ten years ago I had to use the services of a solicitor regarding a very serious matter. The first time I went to their premises I asked to break down the cost of everything they were going to do for me, but I only received a reassuring legal jargon reply. My case was assigned to a young and pretty female. Every time I contacted them by email or phone I asked to start paying because I did not want to receive a massive final bill, and since they were no complying, I sent them a cheque for x pounds. The young and pretty solicitor made a mess of my case, then as I expected I was presented with a massive bill.

In the bill it was mentioned that if I was unhappy I could complain to the Law court, which adjudicated between solicitors and clients. Of course, I did, and won the case against my own solicitor. The Law court confirmed that the bill was extortionate, especially since the firm had never provided me with a breakdown of their costs. I received by post a substantial cheque. Then a week later I received a letter with another cheque and a few explanatory lines. 'Dear Mister Longhi, in recalculating how much we owed you we realised we still owed you £ 50 (enclosed). But in future if you need a solicitor, please go somewhere else. As if I had not already decided so!

I was still living on a 3rd floor in Streets Corner, when I started looking for a house to buy. I went looking on a 20 miles radius from Walsall, but after months of searching I decided to buy a flat in Walsall. Ladypool Close is made of a row of 15 maisonettes, each one with an independent entrance door. The main reason I chose it is for its location: ten yards off the Lichfield Road, about a mile from the town centre and with, opposite my front door, on the other side of Lichfield Road there is Park Lime Pits, a park containing pools, a canal, and a couple of pubs. The park is managed by Walsall Council and it offers plenty of walks. At the back there is the disused Walsall to Lichfield Railway line, ideal for walks. I made an offer a few thousands pound lower than the asking prices and was refused, I made another one and it too was refused. The estate agent told me the owner did not want to come down at all from the asking price, and it was going to put it back on the market soon. I agreed to pay the asking price. I had enough money in the Halifax bank and I could have paid it all in cash, but I did not want to invest nearly all my cash in bricks and mortar once again, so I asked my bank, the Halifax for a £ 30.000 mortgage. At the time I was still working, and my wages went straight into my Halifax account. The mortgage manager noticed my age and knew I could retire within a year, so started asking me all sorts of guarantees. First of all, a letter from the Estate agents where I was renting, declaring that I had always paid my rent on time. I asked if she had ever checked my account, because for the last twelve months there had been a £ 500 direct debit sent to the letting agent, but she insisted on a letter. But once she had the letter from the letting agent she also wanted a letter from a guarantor. I asked why I needed a guarantor, since my cash was in a Halifax account, and the best guarantee was not a piece of paper, but the knowledge that I could not default the mortgage payments, because in the Halifax there was plenty of my money. True I could have closed my accounts, but they could have repossessed the maisonette that was valued much more than £ 30,000. Still they wanted a guarantor and I found it. The next request was a projection of my Italian pension, because the Halifax wanted to be sure I could repay the mortgage once I became a pensioner. It was as if they had not taken any notice of what I have just written in the last two sentences, and every time I fulfilled their request, they moved the goalpost. I explained that dealing with Italian bureaucracy is a nightmare, to no avail. I phoned INPS in Rome, and of course INPS does not accept requests over the phone, even if you live in Timbuktu.

I made a big song and dance having to go to Rome just to obtain a pension projection, I omitted that I went to Rome on holiday twice a year. So, I went to Rome on a holiday cum business. As I expected the office where I had to go was the epitome of chaos and inefficiency. For all the population of Rome and for all the Romans resident abroad there were only two counters open: one for all those whose surname started between A and L, and the other one for those from M to Z. But in order to be called to the counter, everyone had to take a 'numeretto' or little number from a machine and then wait for his number to be called. The residents of Rome must have started queuing outside the building since dawn, in order to get the first 'numeretti'. I am sure Dante would have compared his 'Inferno' or hell, unfavourably to what was happening in that room. People shouting and swearing, one could not hear what the last number called was, an old lady had passed out in the heat and noise of that room. At last my number was called and I asked for my pension projection, but would you believe it, the computer started malfunctioning. After having waited about half an hour for the computer to be revived, I grabbed my projection and left that hall feeling like Chamberlain felt when he was showing to the Brits and the world the piece of paper he got from the Nazis.

In order to speed up the process because I was getting worried the maisonette would be put back on the market, I went in an office and faxed the projection to the Halifax Walsall branch. The day after I arrived back in Walsall I put on my best suit and went to the Halifax fully expecting the mortgage to have been approved. Instead I was told the Bank was referring my request to its underwriters. I asked to be received immediately by the general manager. He did not receive me in his office but in the entrance hall, I asked what was wrong with my mortgage application since I had banked with the Halifax from the day I came to live in Walsall, adding that referring my request to the underwriters was pathetic and ridiculous, I was only going to buy a flat, not Buckingham Palace. He replied that the Bank considered me a bad investment, 'Then why I was asked to produce a dozen of documents, wasting time and money, since the Bank had already decided not to grant me the mortgage, I will tell you why, because you knew that if I did not get the mortgage I would take my savings somewhere else, and that is exactly what I will do now.'

I went out and called in three banks next to the Halifax, and they all offered me a mortgage on the spot, the only proviso being that I banked with them, and when I started producing all the documentation I had with me, they all replied 'We do not need anything, because if you default, we will repossess. Have a good day.' I got a ten years mortgage which I repaid in four years. I referred the matter to the banking Ombudsman and he adjudicated in my favour, within three months I got a £ 200 cheque to cover for my expenses and a letter of apology from the Halifax.

Three years ago, I had decided to go on my first cruise. I saw a discounted cruise advertised, sailing from Southampton and landing at Cadiz, Lisbon and Gibraltar. I emptied my bank account and went. I was hoping to meet a wealthy widow and after having charmed her, leave on her estate in a tropical paradise. I had not realised that the main event on cruise ships was the five daily meals, and that is why I had never seen so many huge bellies in my life. So, to avoid joining the potbellied, every day I went to the gym and walked twice around the ship, that was advertised as one mile in length.

I enjoyed the high-quality evening entertainment very much and the trips ashore, were I could practice my Spanish and Portuguese. But there was a problem: my shower did not work, it was delivering either cold or very hot water, and that caused a problem when in the evening I would join my table wearing a tuxedo. I complained to reception and I was assured the problem would be solved presto. But the morning after having lathered I switched the shower on, and I had to have a cold shower. I carried on complaining on a daily basis, but it was obvious that among the underpaid third world crew members there was not an electrician who could change a thermostat. Reception even suggested I went to the top deck in my robe and had a shower in the bathroom next to the swimming pool! I had to explain to my fellow diners that usually I did not smell that bad, to which a lady said, 'The wc in our cabin does not flush.'

'And have you complained about it?'

'Well.... not yet.'

The conversation went on other topics, thanks God. My bad odour also prevented me from joining the dances in the ballroom, in a nutshell it spoiled my cruise. Then when I went to pay my bill, there was another surprise, £ 45 was added to my bill as 'voluntary gratuity'.

Once I was back home I complained in writing to P&O, and I received a sympathetic letter from them, offering as compensation a £ 100 voucher, redeemable on my next P&O cruise. I could not help smiling when I replied,

'Dear Miss, what makes you think that after the shower ordeal I was subjected to in my first P&O cruises I will book another P&O cruise, bearing also in mind that the author of your brochure confused the adjective obligatory with voluntary? And you are offering me a £ 100 voucher, when for a company sailing the seven seas using an underpaid crew, and supplementing their pay with 'voluntary' tips from the clients, it is the proverbial drop in the ocean?'

'I am offering you a £ 200 cheque then.'

'I will accept nothing less than £ 300 plus a refund of my voluntary tip.'

'£ 250 plus a £ 45 refund.'

'Done.'

To show that I bear no grudges I still have a small current account with the Halifax and have booked a Caribbean Cruise with P&O in January 2018. I was surprised P&O accepted my booking, I thought I would have been blacklisted under the heading 'Complaining smelly Italian'.

About 10 years ago I had bought from the local Peugeot dealer a Peugeot 206 sprint. It had been owned by the dealership and used by its manager for 8 months, so low mileage and almost mint condition. It was an excellent car with a fantastic acceleration which suited an Italian driver. I was a very happy owner for 8 years, then it developed a fault, it was misfiring and losing power, until then I had never had any problem with it. A friend of mine suggested I took it to a garage where he had his car serviced, because it was cheap but good. I was going to go on holiday to Corfu' for a week so I told the garage manager he had a week to fix the car. After a week I went to the garage and found my car with the bonnet open "I was waiting for your return" the garage manager said "Because it needs a new radiator and head gasket". I gave the ok and left. A few days later I received a call that my car was ready for collection, payment in cash.

I know that quite a few traders avoid some tax by not declaring all their income, so I agreed, but when I paid I asked for a receipt which would also have been a guarantee for the work done, but I was refused and the manger said that his word was his bond.

At this point I had realised there was something wrong, but the job had been done, so I paid and left. Only a few days later I noticed water on the floor of the passenger seat, I opened the bonnet and could not see any leak, so I took it back to the garage. The owner told me he knew what was wrong, so I left it again. In the mean time I had to use buses and taxis. Once more I was called to collect my car. I was told that the leak was from the Matrix (a box that sends engine heat into the car), and I had to pay again for that job. Once again cash only, and like Del Boy in Only Fools and Horses, no VAT no guarantee. At home I saw that there still was water on the passenger seat, so guess what? I had to take it back again. This time the manager told me he would install a new Matrix (I thought he had already done it), and would I leave the car... I lost my patience and started arguing with him, but he sweetened the pill by offering me a taxi ride back home. I went one more time to collect the car, and after a few days there is warning on the dashboard telling me "Stop, danger". You would guess it by now, I went back to the garage. The manager had a look and since he could not see anything wrong, he told me he would run diagnostics. Diagnostics did not find anything wrong with the car, so I had to pay and go home still with the warning on the dashboard, and to make my day completely happy, I noticed the leak on the passenger seat had started again. At this point I decided to go to the Peugeot dealership where I had bought the car, I did not go there in the first place because private garages are a lot cheaper than dealerships. They ran diagnostics and found that the warning light was on because there was no brakes fluid, and if had to brake hard I would have had an accident. Then they did change the Matrix, and showed the old one to me, the mechanic had sealed the leak with sealant which with the heat from the engine would eventually melt. I had to pay Peugeot £ 820. But they wrote a report explaining all the failures of that garage and gave me the old Matrix to keep as evidence should I decide to take him to court. That was music for my ears, I immediately downloaded a small claims court form and sued him. In the small claims Court, you can sue anybody for up to £ 6000, all you have to pay is a small fee and eventually court costs if the claim goes to a court judgment and I, the defendant, lost the case.

Time went on and I received from the Court a copy of a letter the Court had received from the garage Manager. In it he described his business as" A small friendly local garage which had never been in trouble before (I was nearly weeping), and myself as a chap who sues everybody in any case, as my friend had told him." I replied to the Court that the small friendly garage had an owner who only accepted cash, did not give receipts, and was also stupid because in accepting my suit he had accepted that I had been his client, because till then thee was no proof. I was furious with my friend who with that stupid remark was giving credence to the owner of the small friendly local garage. Time went on again and one day I received a call from the Court, it was somebody trying to convince me to settle out of Court, because if I lost I would have to pay costs and so on; he also mentioned that the garage manager had offered £ 400 to settle out of Court (thus admitting his guilt). I replied that I wanted the £ 820 I had paid Peugeot to the last penny and if he paid promptly I would not sue him also for the money I had paid him. The Court Clerk went back to the garage manager and 15 minutes later came back to me telling me that I would soon receive a cheque for the full amount. The cheque arrived and would you believe it, it did not bounce!! But sadly, he must have damaged my Peugeot irremediably, because it started leaking oil from the head gasket which he was supposed to have changed and water from the radiator which he also should have changed. I had the head gasket changed from another garage, but the oil leak did not stop. So, since the car still had a fantastic acceleration, I decided to keep it and bought at wholesale prices engine oil and radiator water, and every month I would top both up. But in November 1917 I had to take it this time to a real friendly local garage, and I was told it needed another new head gasket. I knew it would not cure the problem because most cars in their life have only on head gasket change or none at all, and that would have been the third time. I got in my beloved Peugeot for the last time and drove it to the Peugeot dealer I had bought it from, which happened to be also a FIAT dealer. I explained what had happened and asked the bright young man who was serving me that I wanted another nearly new car. He took me out and showed me three Fiat Panda. I tried them all, chose one and paid for it. I asked what he could give me for the Peugeot, he had a very short look at it and offered £ 125, which for a ten-year-old car with 95000 miles on the clock and one mad Italian as previous owner, I thought it was a fair price.

Chapter Seven

Teaching

In order to improve my chances of getting a job I decided to enrol in the local college on a GCSE English, Spanish and Maths. My father-in-law Wilf, at the time was the Education Chairman of Walsall Council, suggested I enrolled on an English course led by Dr Fisher, in his opinion the best in that field. I was already fluent in English, but to prove it to an employer I had to show it in black and white. The course was an Adult Education Evening course, two hours a week.

Dr. Fisher was indeed an excellent teacher, I remember that one day during the lesson he asked me, 'You know Latin, don't you?'

'How do you know?' 'I can tell by the way you construct your English sentences.' It was the first year of the switch from O level to GCSE, and teachers and students alike were not sure on how to carry on with the exam. Anyway, on exam day, I at 49 years of age, sat down in the College hall with 16 years old boys and girls. I got an A. I remember I gave to my father-in-law a copy of the exam paper marked 39 out of 40; Wilf had been born in a very poor Catholic family and at age 13 went to work in the mines. Having had no education to speak of, he made sure that all his children, grandchildren and family relations did. Wilf eventually died, and my wife had the task to dispose of his belongings, and in a draw, she found my exam paper, he had kept it all the time.

At the same time, I enrolled in an adult education elocution class in Queen Mary's Boys, Walsall. The course was led by Douglas Cheadle. Doug had been an engineer and at age 49 had been made redundant, and like me was deemed too old by employers, took early retirement and filled his time as co-ordinator of adult education classes. Knowing my situation, one day he told me 'Antonio the Italian teacher is going back home; would you like to take her place?'

'But I have no experience of teaching.' 'Are you Italian?' 'Yes but....'

'Come with me.' We went to the Italian class and he introduced me to the Italian lady teacher, she briefly told me what topics she had been teaching, and that was it. After a first shaky lesson I realised that not only I could do it, but also that I enjoyed it. At the time no formal qualifications were requested for teaching in Adult Education, as long as you had a working knowledge of the subject   you   were   going   to   teach.

I had never thought to become a teacher, and I owe Doug a huge debt of gratitude because without his introduction to teaching I do not know what I was going to do for the rest of my working years. So, I started looking for other jobs within Adult Education, and when I was teaching at Halesowen College, Birmingham, the Government decided that anybody teaching in the UK should have an UK teaching qualification. Halesowen College were very good to me, they sponsored my course as long as at the end of it I carried on teaching with them.

Once again at age 50 I became a student, teaching part-time and studying part-time. The course was harder than the GCSE, but I had chosen as exam topic, the importance of Latin in the neo romance languages, which was relevant because I intended to become a Modern Languages teacher, and of course I already knew that topic quite well. That was my last chance saloon, If I failed the exam I would have finished the rest of my working life doing odd jobs at the minimum wage. I passed the exam. My teacher phoned me home to tell me the good news and congratulating me for my achievement. She also told me that if I wanted to get all my course work, it was kept in such and such classroom. I went immediately.

Now I started a career as a qualified teacher, mainly in secondary education. As a newly qualified teacher I usually got the worse inner cities schools, where discipline was non-existent. I remember in a school the headmaster telling me not to worry too much about teaching, as long as the classroom was not set on fire.

On the other hand, I remember a school in Aston, inner city Birmingham, where the head mistress told me off for not wearing a tie. I was forced to wear a school tie, as a consequence I was the butt of the jokes from the students. From that day I always kept a spare tie in my car. One of my problems was my name: on entering a classroom for the first time I was asked

'What is your name sir?'

'Longhi'

'Langley?'

'No Longhi'

'Long?'. One day when asked the usual question I replied

'My name is Bond, James Bond' and from that day on I was greeted by 'Good morning Mr. Bond'

When the boys in the classroom realised I was Italian, they wanted to talk about football, which was a good ice breaker, then after 5 minutes I could start the lesson. As a qualified teacher you are supposed to teach any subject in the curriculum. One very cold January morning, with ice on the ground, I reported to reception in my suit and I was given my rota for the day, I noticed that period one was P.E. I said I was not told I was going to teach P.E. otherwise I would have also brought my gym kit. To which the headmaster replied 'But you are not going in the gym, you will play football with the boys. It should not be difficult for you, all Italians love football.' I wanted to reply' Not on a frosty January morning, dressed as a teacher' Instead I went out, took my jacket off and refereed a football match. I was running trying not to fall on the ice, mainly because of my pride, but also to keep warm. Another time I was asked to help the P.E. teacher, and I did, only at the end of the lesson the teacher asked me to go in the girls changing room with a massive torch because the light was not working. It was a terrible strain on my neck.

One year I was teaching in a Walsall school, and during a lesson one boy was continuously teasing me and interfering with my teaching, I gave him two verbal warnings, then I lost my temper, got him from the uniform lapels and shook him a couple of times against the wall. When I released him, he went meekly to his desk, and from that moment I could teach in peace. It was a big risk because if the boy reported my behaviour I would have lost my job. The point is good manners begin at home, and if the parents did not tell their children that the teachers should be respected, when they arrive in a classroom at age 11 to 18, it is far too late to teach them manners.

I remember once I was teaching in the same school, when the lady teacher who was teaching in the classroom next to mine, burst in my classroom and she was very agitated, 'Mr Longhi could you help me please, some students build paper aeroplanes, then set fire to their tips, and aim them at me !!'

Teachers are not allowed to meet with students outside school hours; one day, on a Friday last period, a sixth former pretty girl came to me

'I have lost my bus pass, could you give me a lift home?'

'I am sorry, but if you were a boy I could.'

'Well, if you are that way inclined….' And she turned and went. Occasionally I would enjoy some double entendre using the peculiarities of the English Language. On a Friday last period, usually students are like formula one car drivers waiting for the green light. One day the bell rang, and I pretend not to have heard it, immediately I hear a chorus of

'Sir, sir, the bell has gone !!'

'The bell has gone? Where? I did not see it going. That is a problem we can't go home till the bell rings!'

'No, we meant the bell has rung !!'

'In that case, dismissed.'

Sometimes I have been an invigilator during exams, and at the beginning of the test, among other recommendations we asked the students to deposit their mobiles on a table, and if any student was caught using a mobile during the test, his test would be considered terminated there and then. I could not believe how may mobiles turned up on that table, and how easily at the end of the test the owners found their own on that pile.

Occasionally I was called to teach in denomination schools, were the discipline is very strict. It was like having a day off: when I entered the classroom, they would all get up and greet me. During the lesson nobody would speak unless asked to, I felt like being in a church, it was lovely. One day I was asked to teach Latin in a school where I had never been, it has been the first and the last time of my teaching career. I arrived and walked along manicured lawns and tennis courts. I found my classroom, and I was amazed at the politeness of the students, I had a great teaching day, with no problems at all. When I was leaving I noticed that one of the boys lived in Walsall, so I asked if one of his parents was coming to collect him.

'Sir, we only go home at Christmas, Easter and in the summer, this is a boarding school!'

Occasionally I was asked to teach in primary schools, and that was great. Those children were used to female teachers, and when I entered the classroom they all chanted 'Goood mooorning Miss.' I gave a stern look then in my baritone voice would say 'Do I look like a miss?' 'Oh sorry, goood moorning sir.' Those children saw in me dad or even grandad, it was a pleasure to teach them, the girls would draw hearts on cardboard and with doe eyes asked me' This is for you sir, will you come again tomorrow?'

There is a school in the Dudley area called Tividale. Since it was one of the worst, when I joined the teaching staff it was already in special measures. The staff were very friendly and over the years we started exchanging Christmas cards and presents. The headmaster knowing how troublesome his students were, was on patrol during the lessons. One day, while I was teaching, a massive sixth former opens the door, picks up a desk and throws it to a boy. It only took 30 seconds from beginning to end. I asked a boy to call the headmaster, he comes in and calls an ambulance for the injured student, then tells me to call the police. He goes to the nearest A&E, and I file a police report with a PC who in the meantime had arrived. The day after I was in the staff room and read this on the board: 'For his aggressive behaviour, student XYZ has been disciplined with one-week suspension.' I went to the headmaster and told him that student XYZ had a criminal instinct and should have been expelled from all the schools in the UK for ever, not just for a week. Also, I did not want to carry on teaching in a school where potential criminals were still accepted as students.

He replied 'But Antonio, if I expel all the students who behave badly, only the teaching staff would be left in this school. I do not blame you if you want to leave, I would do the same if I could, but I still have a mortgage to pay and a young family to grow.'

A few months after I left, Tividale comprehensive was closed for good. The discipline problem was getting worse all the time, some schools had installed panic buttons in every classroom, so that in emergency the teacher pressed the button, and Security staff would turn up, and all they asked was 'Which ones?' The teacher would point to the culprits and they were taken away. During the last year of my teaching career, some schools were advertising for ex-service men and policemen, with no teaching qualifications, to become teacher's assistants, with the sole purpose of keeping discipline. This was against all rules, but the Ministry of education closed both eyes. It was a desperate move, which in a way I agreed with, because in some schools I felt better equipped to teach if instead of using pens and dictionaries I wore a bullet proof vest. I always tried to enjoy my teaching days by using humour.

I remember I was teaching in Perry Barr school, Birmingham. One day I was having coffee with an all-female staff in the staff room, when the secretary opens the door and announces, 'The fire brigade has arrived for their demonstration.' Since nobody moved, I got up and went to meet the strapping young firemen. I took them to the staff room, opened the door and introduced them to the shy ladies with 'And now for one day and one day only the fire brigade will perform the full Monty!! Take it away lads !!' And then closed the door behind me.

My last position was with Queen Mary's Girls Grammar in Walsall, where my sister-in-law had been a student, my wife's cousin a teacher and I had gone to parent's evenings when my daughter Laura had been a student. There were no discipline problems, and the staff were lovely. But one day I was called to the headmistress office and I was informed that because of budget reasons, they were dispensing with my services. I went to my classroom and emptied my draws, feeling like mister Chips in the film.

Then I started a private teaching career, I loved it because the majority of my clients were adults who needed to know and wanted to learn the Italian or French language for business, or just because they wanted to speak the local language when on holiday. I also had quite a few children, and in both cases the adults and children came to me because they wanted to learn.

I was advertising on the internet, and I was called by a London school asking me if I was interested in teaching Italian to the manager of Muller dairies, a German multinational company selling yogurt products in Europe. I accepted and started teaching him in his home in Acton Trussell, a lovely village near Stafford. He was a young man in his 30's, with no other language knowledge apart from English, so we started from scratch. He had a day off from work just to do his homework, he was bright and willing to learn, I enjoyed teaching him. He was supposed to go to work in Italy, so that Muller could get a better share of the yogurt business, at the time dominated by other companies. Within six months I took him from zero to the point that he told me 'Antonio, when you give me a DVD to watch in Italian and read the English subtitles in case I can't follow the

Italian dialogue, do not worry about the subtitles, because I can understand everything said.'

I realised my job was done, but he was going to Italy to do business, so I equipped him with the basic tools of doing business in Italy, i.e. when to use a gentle bribe like a box of good wines, or a bunch of flowers if dealing with a woman, or when not to use those methods because they could prove to be counterproductive.

Then he went off to an office in Verona and a villa on nearby lake Garda. Muller headquarters gave me a letter he had sent to the company, congratulating me for having taught him not only the language, but also how to behave in a business environment in Italy.

Chapter 8

More Travels

In the chapter entitled Peculiarities, after having kissed the lady at the till, I left the charity shop and bumped into a man. When I said sorry and he replied to my apology, we recognised each other by our accents as fellow Italians and exchanged telephone numbers. His name was Pietro, born in Sicily. A few days later he invited me to his flat to meet his sister and brother-in-law; it was Christmas time, and he produced a Panettone cake which for Italians is what the Christmas pudding is for the British. Only this beautifully wrapped Panettone had still attached the receipt, Harrods, and its astronomical price. It should have been an alarm bell of his extravagant future behaviour, but I ignored it. Another time he invited me to go to a restaurant, and when I got in his car, I saw that he had had it valeted, and to make sure I noticed it, he had left on the floor the paper. I told him that such pleasantries were not necessary between friends, a friend should be treated in a normal manner, but he was trying to make an impression on me. For the readers to understand Pietro's behaviour I must explain that he was very touchy and arrogant.

He persuaded me to go on holiday with him to Sicily. I thought he would be my guide, proud to show me the beautiful island where he was born. He told me he had worked at Catania airport, omitting to say he was a clerk and worked in an office; the relevance of this observation will be clear soon. Anyway, I arranged the flights, but when it came to choosing the hotel I had to speak to the owner of the hotel, who was of course his friend (he was boasting all the time that he knew important people). Before we left he invited me to his flat for a coffee and a chat, then I realised that he was spending his days on the phone, and the recipients of his calls were enduring his calls out of politeness.

Having booked the hotel and the car, we flew to Catania. On arrival, after collecting the suitcases I wanted to collect the rental car, but he walked so slowly because of his age   that I told him to wait for me. I collected the car and picked him up.

He could not remember how to get to Acitrezza, the seaside village where we had booked the hotel. I started asking for directions, but he took it as a personal offence and started shouting at me. At that point I started shouting louder and told him to shut up. Following road signs, I found Acitrezza.

The day after this we walked into the town centre, at snail's pace, where he met his friends, and at an even slower pace we walked to a bar where we had a typical Sicilian ice-cream (cassata siciliana). Then Pietro wanted to get some cash from the ATM but could not remember his PIN number.

The day after I had to drive him to a bank where he could get some cash. At that point I told him I wanted to see Sicily, Taormina, Mount Etna, and so on, but he replied, 'I am not interested, I have already seen all that.' So, I dropped him to the hotel and started visiting on my own.

First, I went to Taormina, a beautiful town which had been founded by the Greeks, who had built a theatre overlooking the sea. Then another day I went on top of Mount Etna. This volcano is still active and occasionally buries under lava the buildings near the top. The view was amazing and there were no clouds. Since Pietro and I had parted company, occasionally in the evening I would meet Pietro's friends in the town centre where I used to go for my evening meal. One day I was asked, 'Is it true that Pietro can still go to bed with a woman?'

'I do not know, and I do not care, but at over eighty years of age I doubt it.' But one day Pietro rang my room and he wanted me to say hullo to the maid in his room. As if that meant anything; the innuendo was that he was still sexually active.

Anyway, even if he was ruining my holiday, I felt sorry for him, and when he asked me to drive him to Barrafranca, a village in the mountains where all the Italians living in Walsall came from, I agreed fully knowing that there was nothing there to attract a tourist. It was a long drive from Acitrezza, but Pietro made sure I was enjoying it. He gesticulated while I was driving, pointing to the orange groves, and several times I had to put his arms down because he was interfering with my driving. I was nearly a nervous wreck when we arrived at a half way stop, where I could admire in the distance the city of Enna and stretch my legs and go to the loo. We were in this bar sipping coffee when he bought a cannolo, a typical Sicilian cake, very heavy and difficult to digest.

'You must eat this, it is the best in Sicily.'

'But Pietro your sister in Barrafranca is cooking a meal, and I will be eating at your sisters for hours, if I eat that cannolo I will not be able to enjoy your sister's food.'

Since he was insisting I suggested I could eat it later on. In the end I had to shout at him, like you do to a child. So, we arrived in Barrafranca and I understood why everybody preferred Walsall.

Pietro could not find his sister's house, so he phoned her from his mobile, but could not reach her. I asked him to give me his mobile and she answered me. I must now explain that Pietro believed one has to use different mobiles according to where you were, a British one for the UK and an Italian one for Italy. I tried to explain that it was the same, but he would not listen.

As I expected the meal compared favourably with my sister's, so I explained that I would taste every dish, only as a child's portion. When Pietro's sister tried to fill my dish, her daughter, told her to stop. At the end of the meal, as dessert, I was presented with a choice of cannoli and I chose the mini version. Pietro went for a siesta and I tried to explain that Pietro had lots of problems, but the only one who fully understood what I tried to say was the niece, a young Sicilian beauty, because she was young and open minded. Having seen Barrafranca, I do not understand why the people of Barrafranca leave it in order to live and work in Walsall, but when they are dead wanting to be buried in Barrafranca, as the local funeral director can testify.

On the way back, we had to stop to a bakery to buy Sicilian cakes to bring back home. Of course, he knew the owner of the shop, and possibly even the Mayor of that hamlet. I bought my cakes then sunbathed outside while Pietro was reminiscing with the staff.

Another day he begged me to take him to a village where his cousin had an office; he had to see him on business. And off we went. It was a pretty village, and after the usual stop in the bar where, you could guess it by now, he knew the owner, we agreed that I would have lunch while he went to his cousin. I also added that I saw a road sign indicating Bronte, and I wanted to go there because of the connection with the UK. Pietro started shouting that I was supposed to wait for him, and I left the bar while he was still shouting.

I had a beautiful lunch basking in the sunshine, and I conversed with the owner of the restaurant. He told me that the village was Mafia territory, and he was one of the few entrepreneurs who had refused to leave the village. He was not paying the 'pizzo' or a percentage of his profits to the Mafia and knew that sooner or later the Mafia would do something about it. I then headed towards Bronte and stopped in a village famous for growing pistachio nuts. After having asked for directions I found an unbelievable shop: apart from selling pistachio in its natural state, it also sold pistachio coffee, bread, pasta, jam and marmalade, olive oil, cheese and only God knew what else. I bought two half kilo packs and tasted some coffee, then left. I found my car where I had left it, but before resuming my journey I needed a drink, so I entered in a bar and I asked for a drink and for directions to the Bronte estate, and the lady at the bar gave me a road map for free. I wanted to buy something else to show gratitude.

She said, 'You do not have to buy anything, thank you will be enough. But when you go back to the Continent (for Sicilians the Continent means Italy) I would like you to tell that in Sicily we are not all Mafiosi, but also hard-working law-abiding citizens.' I promised to do so, then she discouraged me to proceed to Bronte, since it would be too late to see anything. I opened the map and asked the quickest way back to Acitrezza.

'You are staying in Acitrezza? I am from Acitrezza.'

I told her I could give her a lift back home and asked her to become my guide, but she was living in that village. So back to grumpy Pietro.

At last departure day arrived and I thought the worst of the holiday had gone, but I was in for a surprise. As usual Pietro pretended to remember the way to Catania airport. Once I had found my way there, I told him that because of his walking problem, I was giving him his boarding card and all he had to do was to go to check in and have it validated with the correct gate number. I in the meantime would give the car back to the rental company and would meet him either at the check-in desks or at the gate. I went back to the airport and found Pietro in deep conversation with a very young check-in woman.

'So, you do not know the Airport Director, Dr YXZW?' Pietro was saying.

I intervened, 'Pietro you must have finished working about 40 years ago, she must be in her 20's, how could she know him? The director you knew could even be dead by now! I will see you at gate eight.' I had wanted to stop that ridiculous conversation.

'And where is gate eight?'

'Between seven and nine.'

I went to the gate. I was pretending not to know him, but when he found me he proclaimed to all the people at gate eight, 'This is my friend Antonio. I know that deep down he likes me!' He meant that even if I was ignoring him and keeping 10 metres away, we were friends; I was very embarrassed, and that never happens.

We landed at Birmingham airport in the evening, and I had booked a taxi to get us back home. Once we both were in the airport I gave him these instructions, 'Since I will be at the luggage carousel much earlier than you, I will collect both my suitcase and yours, go to the toilet and change into warmer clothes, then I will wait for you by the toilet.' I waited by the toilet for ages, all the passengers on our flight had collected their luggage and had gone, but no sign of Pietro. Then I rang his Italian mobile, no reply, his English mobile, no reply. I could not go back to look for him because I had already passed passport control. The taxi I had booked called me to say he was ready to pick me up. I asked to wait a few more minutes, but he pointed out that since he had other bookings either I went there and then, or he would go. I gave another look around, then went. I went to his flat and left his luggage by his door, then went home.

I half expected him to phone me to explain what had happened, but his wounded pride would not let him do it. A week later I phoned him to make sure he was ok.

'Hi Pietro, Antonio speaking, how are you?'

'I do not know any Antonio.'

Thinking back some situations were farcical, but not if you were involved in the farce.

During the last few years I have taken to Rome some of my Italian language students. I organised the flights, hotels, car rental etc.

One year I remember that only one student could come, and since I would go to Rome in any case to visit my sister and friends, off we went. Chas and I had a good time, because she was willing to accept my daily suggestions of where to go. I did not have to negotiate with other students who had already been there or wanted to see something else.

The first day I will not forget, I took her to see one of Rome's four Cathedrals, St. Paul's outside the Walls. I knew it very well because my family had moved from near St. Peter's to near St. Paul's. In my opinion St. Paul's is the most beautiful of the four Cathedrals, its façade is inlaid with golden mosaics, and when the sun sets its rays reflect on the façade and create a show of glittering beauty. Once inside, the nave is ornate all the way around with pictures of all the Popes, from St. Peter's to the actual one. Legend says that when there are no more spaces for another picture, that will be the end of the world. There were only three spaces left. We walked towards the altar, and a Mass was on with choir singing. We stopped for the Mass. I turned to Chas and I saw she was crying. I asked what was the matter and she told me, 'Antonio I am ok, I am only overwhelmed by the beauty of it all.'

Next, I took her to the Cimitero degli Inglesi, the English cemetery. For the Italians all non-Catholics were English, hence its name. Since they could not be buried in consecrated soil, a special place was dedicated for their burial. It is situated next to the Piramede Cestia, the only Pyramid built for burial outside Egypt. Caius Cestius was a very rich merchant at the time of the Roman Empire, and he thought that once he was dead nobody would remember him, because he was not an emperor or general. He decided to be buried in a pyramid like a Pharaoh, and his sarcophagus is inside the Pyramid. On certain days of the week it is possible to visit the Pyramid. The Cemetery, however, is open every day, there is no fee to enter, but a donation is accepted for feeding and looking after all the cats who do a fantastic job in keeping vermin at bay around all of Rome's monuments. We went in and on the left, there is the burial monument of the poet Keats. Chas was very interested of course. Hundreds of people of all religions are buried here. We were walking around when a lady approached us.

'Are you staying for the concert?'

I did not know about it but accepted the invitation. So, we sat under pines, the sun shining on us, with as background the Pyramid, and listened to a classical music concert.

Another day I took her to Villa Borghese, which was donated by the Borghese family to the people of Rome. It has become Rome's biggest park, it is so big that inside there is also Rome's zoo, and Piazza di Spagna, a place dedicated to horse riding, a lake where you can hire a boat and take your companion on the lake, the Villa Borghese itself, a palace housing a museum of classical art, various fine buildings where you can dine or have a coffee in style, and il Pincio, a place where you can admire all of Rome at your feet. Chas and I walked a lot, it was a very hot October day and I took my shirt off and sunbathed on a bench. She welcomed the stop because her feet were giving her problems.

On other trips I took my party to the town of Marino, situated on the hills around Rome, or Castelli Romani. The area is dotted with picturesque towns every few miles, Frascati, Marino, Albano, Castelgandolfo overlooking the lake sharing its name, famous for the summer Papal residence, Nemi and a few more. This is a wine growing region and every town produces its own wine. On the first Sunday in October Marino celebrates its wine by La Festa del Vino, or wine festival. The town's public fountains will pour for twenty-four hours wine instead of water. I try not to miss it because Marino's wine is amazingly good: it is a delicate white, not too strong, and when you drink it you want to drink more because it goes down without giving the impression you are drinking alcohol. I invariably get happy on it, and here are a few anecdotes.

One year having drunk my quota, I was having a siesta on a bar chair, when I heard a whistle. In my slumber I thought I were at a football match and the ref had given a penalty. I finally woke up altogether and was met by a traffic policeman in his white uniform 'Is that car yours?

'Yes, why?

'Because you have parked it in a no parking area, and I always whistle before affixing a fine on the windscreen, so that if the owner removes it I do not fine him. But now it is too late.'

'I am sorry, are you sure you can't forget about the fine? I am from Rome but live in England, and every year I bring a party to Marino, to taste your delicious wine and porchetta (roast pork)'

. He told me to follow him in his office.

'You see, not only you should not have parked there, but you parked in my own spot, and I am the chief of police!' Then he got the fine and shredded it. 'But now remove your car and do not tell the locals what I have done.'

Another year I was supposed to drive a minibus full of students and my wife Jo back to the hotel in Rome, but Jo realised I was not fit for the purpose, so she pushed me into a bar to have a few strong coffees to reverse the effect of the wine. I entered wearing my Roma football cap. I ordered a strong coffee, but before I could drink it the barwoman noticed my cap and exclaimed, 'You are a Roma fan like me!' and as usual I could not refrain from hugging and kissing her. Jo was in a fury and I could not understand why!

Every winter in order to break the long British winter, I take a holiday in a hot country. In winter because of the bad operation to my nose, I suffer from a perennial cold and cough, which stops me from singing altogether. While if I am for a few days in a hot dry climate, my chest clears, and my overall health improves. I went to Agadir for the first time in 2014. Agadir, on the Moroccan Atlantic coast, was completely destroyed by an earthquake in the early 50's. It has been rebuilt with taste and it offers a warm climate, unspoilt beaches, cheap but good accommodation and tasty food. In the evening there is plenty of entertainment, notably belly dancing. I was looking for a local travel agent and found a small one just across the road from my hotel. It was manned by a young man, Brahim. I can speak a decent French, but he preferred to speak in English. He opened his heart to me and told me his story of survival in a country ruled by a benign monarch, but with no social security, hardly any work and no national health service. He came to Agadir from a village in the Atlas Mountains, where his parents were sustenance farmers and their biggest asset was a cow. One day we went to a similar village and I was touched by the extreme poverty. The main mode of transport was donkeys, and children in the streets were trying to sell us little hand painted stones. The agency was owned by an Irish lady who had married a Moroccan and settled down in Agadir. Her husband was serving a prison sentence, I did not ask what for. That is why Brahim had found that job. I befriended Brahim, who was a naïve young man, and tried to help him. He was in love with a Moroccan girl living in Paris but had not told her. In his job there were plenty of occasions to meet other girls, Moroccan and Europeans, but he was saving himself for the girl in Paris. I booked a few trips with his agency. I explained to Brahim that if he married the girl in Paris he would acquire French nationality and could find work in France, leaving behind the precarious living he was forced to do. He had no living quarters to speak of, and when I mentioned I would like to send him some money, he said, 'Do not send cash, where I live people can smell cash in an envelope."

I asked Mary, the Irish lady owner what I could do to help him, and she said he badly needed to go to a dentist but could not afford it. So, I gave him £ 20, which when changed in local currency became more than enough for the dentist. And with £ 20 I made someone happy, if only it could be that easy all the time.

One day I had booked through the local rep a trip to the legendary Marrakesh. I, and other people in my party, were not entirely sure of its location, so in the morning we boarded the coach wearing flips flops, shorts and a t shirt. In Agadir the day time temperature would easily reach 38c. A huge alarm bell rung when I saw that the driver was dressed in skiing gear, and a massive one when I realised that the coach was steadily climbing altitude. We stopped half way for toilets, and it was painfully cold. When we arrived in Marrakesh we noticed that everyone was dressed for an alpine expedition rather than going to the beach. Marrakesh in winter is a ski resort in the Atlas Mountains, and in about three hours we went from 35c to about 10.

Marrakesh is worthwhile a visit, its souk is enormous, and without a guide it would have been impossible to come out. In order to keep warm, we were sipping hot drinks all the time. We visited a fantastic palace, with internal gardens and fountains, ornate by mosaics and paintings. After lunch we had free time, and in the main square there were snake charmers, musicians, performing monkeys. When the sun set the temperature went down to near freezing, so all those wearing beach gear congregated in a bar which had a couple of gas heaters, but the doors wide open. I went to talk to the guide and suggested that since we had seen everything there was to be seen, and since we were near freezing temperature while dressed for the beach, could we start going back right away rather than wait till 2000. And his answer was no. So, we carried on sipping mint tea and huddling nearer to the gas heater. I thought I was getting frostbite.

As soon as I was back in the UK I wrote a letter of complaint to the travel agent, explaining that the local rep should have warned us to dress properly, and the guide should at least have taken us back earlier. After the customary denial of guilt from the travel agent, I referred the matter to ABTA who forced the agency to compensate me. I forgot the amount, but it would never have compensated me for the cold I suffered during that trip.

The year after there was a big upsurge of terrorist activities nearly everywhere, I emailed Brahim asking if Morocco was still safe. Having received a positive answer, I went to Agadir again. The meeting with Brahim was quite emotional. The moment the Moroccan husband of the Irish lady was released from jail, he sacked Brahim, who then went for a while to his parent 's village, till he found a job on a boat which took tourists on day trips. I booked a trip and saw Brahim working as chef, waiter, cleaner and doing anything that was required for the smooth running of the trip. In return he would get a small wage and permission to sleep on board at night. In 12 months, he had grown in confidence and did not talk any more of his idealistic love for the girl in Paris; in short, he had become a man.

One day I asked him to have lunch with me in my hotel, and even he for security reasons had to show his ID to reception. During the day the beaches were patrolled by soldiers wearing full uniform and holding a Kalashnikov rifle. It was a reassuring albeit scary sight. One evening I was having dinner in the hotel restaurant, when I heard a voice asking me if it could sit at my table. I raised my gaze and saw the owner of the voice, a woman wearing a miniskirt and in her early 40's, and I immediately accepted her at my table. We introduced ourselves to each other; her name was Shirley and she told me she was a French singer touring the various hotels where she was engaged to sing, and she lived in my hotel. I told her I was a singer of sorts, and we had a couple of duets in French. Then she went to sing in the hotel night club; she sang beautifully, but the audience was noisy and did not pay her much attention. I do not know why with all the younger males in the hotel she had chosen to sit at my table, but thinking of Brahim, I saw it as a God sent opportunity. My plan was for the two to meet and who knows, there may be a sparkle. So, I booked another boat trip and invited Shirley to come along, but in the morning, she did not turn up. I mentioned Shirley to Brahim and he replied with the usual fatalistic, 'In sh Allah.'

The morning after, I was leaving, and Shirley turned up apologising for having missed the trip. She had been asked to sing in a hotel too far away to return on time. She asked the waiter to take pictures of us together, then I had to leave. I have kept in touch with both Brahim and Shirley by email, and occasionally by phone. I am happy to have been able to help Brahim, a young, polite, well mannered, human being.

Years ago, my son Marco decided to have a family holiday. That year he booked a flat in a refurbished farm in the centre of France in July. Jo and I, Marco and his wife Andrea with their two little daughters, went to Le Havre by car and ferry. We had rented a car to be picked up in Le Havre and driven it to our flat. In Le Havre the man at the car rental only spoke French and I expected him to speak English also because the ferry was full of Brits. I managed to make myself understood and we drove off. That was a very hot summer and about 25.000 elderly people died in France. We had a good time visiting castles, villages and local markets. All my family was always near me because after a few days all the French I knew came back to me, and I was called as an interpreter all the time. There were farmers living and working around us, and one evening they invited us to an al fresco chat and drinking session. They had brought outdoors a fridge full of drinks. They started offering us the local beer, then carried on with the wine produced by them. At that point I started feeling happy and decided not to drink any more. The farmers opened a bottle of Calvados and were filling our glasses, but I without being noticed emptied my glass and any more glasses in a pot, and the plant in it wilted. Marco carried on drinking, but Andrea does not drink alcohol at all and Jo knew when to stop. In The morning I was the only one up, I got on a bike and went in the nearest village boulangerie where I bought croissants and baguettes for breakfast. When I arrived back Marco was still nursing a head ache but a strong coffee and the smell of the freshly baked croissants soon revived him.

I have travelled much more, but this book it is not a book only about my travels, so I am going to stop here....

Chapter Nine

More travels

I had moved to Walsall in February 1966 and stayed in an old cottage near the Arboretum park. The elderly landlady did not make me pay any rent as long as I painted and repaired it. After having married Jo on July 31st 1966 in St. Patrick's R.C. Church, Walsall, we moved to Rome where I had found a Job with Alitalia, and a perk of the job was free world- wide flights travel on any airline. I had found rooms in a hotel with great difficulty because that day was the day of the world cup final between England and Germany, so I dropped my Italian family in this hotel while on my way to

Heathrow where I was going to fly to Rome and then spend my honeymoon on the Amalfi coast and Ravello.

When God created Heaven, he created Ravello. When I was a teenager I had spent all my summer holidays in Minori a town a few miles from Amalfi and Ravello. But let us go back to my family in a London hotel reception. None of them spoke any English, only my sister Gilda spoke good French. My elderly uncle Attilio had pestered me for hours because he wanted a map of London written in Italian, but in 1966 there were none.

I left them at reception but suddenly I saw their luggage thrown on the pavement. I went back in and because of the language barrier the hotel personnel thought they had no money to pay the bill. I sorted it out. Then when I came back from my honeymoon I heard tales of coffees served in toilets, one day they were going somewhere by underground and my mother Anna and Gilda were the first persons to go down the moving staircases, but my mother had never seen something like that and was terrified, so like a stubborn mule refused to step on it. After several minutes Gilda convinced our mother to go down, in the meantime the British gentlemen in bowler hats, striped suits and the customary umbrella had waited patiently for my mother to move on. When Gilda and my mother arrived on the tube platform and my mother moved out of the way, they lost their composure and hurried to their trains.

After settling down in my job, I told Jo that before starting a family we should go on a long holiday.

Therefore, I collected all my annual holidays, I bought dozens of tickets from Alitalia and many more airlines and off we went. We landed as a first stop in Ceylon, now renamed Shri-Lanka. After a few days we landed in Bangkok and visited all the main sights like the gigantic reclining Buddha, the main temples and dined in a top floor revolving restaurant. From Bangkok we flew on Air New Zealand to Fiji. When we passed through the daytime zone we were given a certificate. In order to catch a flight to Fiji we had to land in Sydney. The Alitalia DC8 was full of elderly Italians who were going to visit their children who had emigrated to Australia many years earlier. Most of them did not speak any English, had never flown before, had never left their villages; when the cabin staff produced the food, they refused it thinking they had to pay, instead from their bags produced wine and cut bread into salami and prosciutto ham sandwiches, and started singing the songs of their regions.

Before landing the cabin staff handed landing cards, and of course not only they could not read the English, some could not read at all, so I offered to help them. I asked the addresses of the places where they were going to stay and very few stayed in Sydney, the majority had to travel to villages inland, and unless they were met by their relatives at the airport they would never have reached their destinations. I had to admire the courage and bravery of those elderly mothers and fathers. We were going to Fiji on the invitation of Oscar Emberson, a dentist who had worked with Jo in Walsall, and after marrying a Walsall lady he decided he had enough money to go back to Fiji and open a dentist practice, treating the locals for free and making the tourist pay. He was a member of the royal family of Tonga, and as such he had a servant and a body guard who would sleep outside his bedroom. We were his guests at Christmas time in his house on the beach. In his garden grew banana trees, palms and tropical plants. The only problem was that in Fiji mosquitos are the size of helicopters and thrive on mosquito repellent creams, so at night we slept under a mosquito net, with one fan at the bottom of the bed and one at the top, moving off mosquitos trying to get in the net.

One day Oscar invited me to shop in the local fruit and veg market. I was mesmerised by the abundance, variety and size of everything; I picked up a bananas bunch weighing a ton and asked Oscar to take it home, he had a look at the price tag and exclaimed, "What? Fifty cents? Too expensive, put it down."

One day I noticed about 20 men wearing prison uniform walking escorted only by a policeman whose weapon was not a gun but a baton. I asked Oscar why the prisoners did not escape "And where would they go? Sharks are waiting for them on the other side of the barrier reef, look around and you will see people with an arm or a leg missing."

Another day I was walking along the beach and saw a dozen women standing in shallow water in a circle, wearing large gowns. Suddenly in unison they join the gowns and slowly walked to the centre of the circle, at the same raising the gowns who had become a fishing net. When they touched each other raised the gowns out of the water and caught dinner. Such was the abundance of flora and fauna that the majority of people do not use cash. There is a rush to become citizens of one of these tropical islands, and governments have imposed rigid quotas.

Another day we went on a fishing trip, towards a tiny island where we would cook and eat the fish. After a while I caught a medium size fish, but Oscar confiscated it." You see Antonio the fish here are not used to fishermen and they bite at everything, but if I use this fish as bait we will catch even more'. And so it was.

Christmas day arrived, and Oscar and his family pretended to be in Europe or the US where is winter, and decorated Christmas trees with snow, sang Christmas carols and so on. The main course for lunch was a roasted piglet. The servants dug a hole in the garden and heated big stones on a wood fire, when the stones were very hot they were placed in the hole, then the piglet is wrapped in banana leaves and placed in the hole, more hot stones cover the piglet and then soil was placed to cover the piglet. This contraption becomes a slow-cooker, roasting the animal to perfection not letting escape a drop of juice or any aroma.

On the way to the US we had to fly back to Nandi international airport, on the other side of the island. We flew the 30 minutes trip on an 8-seater plane forgotten there by the Wright brothers, we had to cross a mountain ridge that divided the island into two halves. At Nandi we boarded a flight to Los Angeles, but when we arrived we realised that our suitcases had been left back in Nandi. We were not terribly worried because in the city of angels it was quite warm and sunny.

We stayed in a downtown hotel, and we visited the original Disneyland. I loved it because I grew up reading the Disney cartoons featuring Mickey Mouse, Goofy, Donald Duck and Pluto the dog. It was an incredible experience and I am sure the children that visited it did not appreciate the amount of state-of-the-art technology behind every attraction. We visited the stand of the American typical household, and in the early 70's the American kitchen was already equipped with microwave ovens and other appliances that would reach the old world at least 15 years later. We also went on a trip to Beverley Hills where we were shown the luxurious houses of actors and singers, then we went on to Hollywood for a tour of the film studios. I remember visiting a zoo of some sort where all the animals who starred in films were kept. Another day we went to the Chinese Theatre where all the hand-prints of famous actors are embedded in concrete slabs. After a few days we flew a short trip to Las Vegas on a DC9 two jet engine plane. Before landing the pilot informed us that we were landing using one engine only and that was the only flight of the many I flew before and after where there was any real danger.

We stayed at the Flamingo hotel and all the hotels rooms and food were cheap because the hotels made their money on the gambling. We saw shows performed by singers like Connie Francis and Frank Sinatra junior. One evening we walked all the famous Strip and briefly visited the most important hotels on both sides. The one that left an indelible impression in my memory was Caesar's Palace, all made with Carrara white marble imported from Italy. All the staff wore Roman dress, it was an incredible sight. At the time Caesar's Palace hosted nearly all boxing world titles, and they were beamed on TV screens across the world.

We had a look at a chapel where one could phone a vicar and get married during a short ceremony which in the price included the organ music and the services of two witnesses. Before the trip to Las Vegas I did not know I had married a gambling addict, Jo would spend hours on games that we could afford, mainly the one arm bandits. At the time I did not have plastic money, so the day before leaving I went to a bank asking to change a 10 thousand lire banknote into dollars. The note was as big as a page of a tabloid newspaper, and when I gave it to a bemused bank employee he had a good look and then asked, "What is this?" I explained that it was Italian legal tender. He had a good look and then phoned his main office to be reassured I was not having him on. With those few dollars and with our winter clothes still left in our luggage in Fiji, we embarked on a flight to New York. We arrived on a January day and we were welcomed by a snow blizzard and very low temperatures. In order not to freeze to death I spent some dollars in Macey's store in order to buy two plastic macs. And braving the cold we went on top of the Empire State skyscraper, to Ellis Island where all immigrants were inspected for signs of bad health, and some had to go back to their countries.

We also went inside the Statue of Liberty and walking on a spiral staircase. I spotted the picture of an immigrant woman dressed in a typical black top and gown, she was holding a baby in her arms and was looking at the camera with a gaze that meant, "I have made it!"

And so back to Rome, still wearing the same clothes. Working at the airport I managed to trace our suitcases back in a couple of weeks.

A trip I make every year is to the Edinburgh Tattoo. I have been several times to Scotland and the weather has always been dry and sunny. The Edinburgh Tattoo is a celebration of military bands and folk groups coming to Edinburgh every August. The audience patiently queus for a long-time outside Edinburgh Castle waiting to find their seats, and at dusk the show starts, it usually is televised on the BBC. For nearly three hours I have enjoyed an amazing performance of military bands playing and parading, folk groups dancing, usually the bands and folk groups come from the Commonwealth. It ends with fireworks and pipers playing "For all long sine" and the audience holding hands and singing together. I go to the Tattoo by coach and the coach company includes in the trip visits to castles and nearby cities like Fort William.

It is very strange why in Edinburgh there is the biggest concentration of Italians in the UK. The immigration started last century, often the immigrants walking from the poorest Italian regions all the way up to Scotland. Historians could not explain why they did not stop and settle down in the nearer and warmer south of England. I feel at home in Edinburgh because every single restaurant and bar is owned by Italians still speaking Italian, with a few exceptions. Every year I pay a visit to a shop called "Valvona and Crolla", which was founded in 1934, and since then has been selling Italian food, wine and liqueurs to the Italian community and to the British at large. Nowadays it sells online too of course. If I do not remember their exact location I pop in any Italian bar, ask for directions and find their premises. It is made of a long corridor, on one side there is food, on the other side wine and drinks, usually there are Italians ladies shopping for food as if they were in their village in Italy. The first time I went I asked for a bottle of Cynar, an Italian liqueur, and the man who was serving me apologised because he loved Cynar, but he could not even find it for himself, so I bought a bottle of Amaro Averna. Back to Walsall I went on Amazon website and bought a bottle of Cynar which was delivered to my flat within days.

I believe Amazon could sell freezers to the Eskimos and apart from their practice of paying low wages and avoiding paying taxes in the UK, it is an amazing business. The year after I went back to Valvona and Crolla and that time they had plenty of Cynar. I love Scotland and the Scots, the only thing I dislike is their insistence on flogging their pounds to the tourists. Many times, paying something in cash, I got the change in Scottish pounds, I refused it and they explained that it is legal tender. I retort it may be legal tender in Scotland, but once over the border nobody accepts it, it is like Monopoly money. And if it is legal tender why don't they keep it and instead try to get rid of it? In the end I got the change in English pounds.

Chapter Ten

Odds and Ends

In this chapter I am going to write about episodes of my life I could not fit in anywhere else.

My sister Gilda used to tell me that our father had only one hobby: AS Roma football club. Not having a son to take to matches he took her instead and my poor sister had to endure this situation while she would have rather been with her friends. When I was old enough to go to matches, my father died, I was five years old. So, Roma is in my blood as it was in my father's, but when I started having boys to take to matches, they became fans of the other Rome football club, Lazio. Fortunately, Gilda had a son, Maurizio who had married another Roma fan, Rossella, and we started going to matches together. It was and it still is customary that when your side scores everyone jumps and hugs friends and any other fan nearby.

I was already living in Walsall but occasionally I would go to the Stadio Olimpico in Rome with Maurizio and Rossella. In this occasion he had asked me to buy the tickets at a tobacconist(?) in Viale Aventino not far from where I used to live. I went there in my rented car but could find parking only at a bus stop and knowing I would only be away about five minutes, I took the risk. The tobacconist only accepted cash, so I went to a couple of nearby ATMs but I could not get any cash, therefore I went to get the cash inside a bank. All this took about half an hour and when I went to the car I found it dangling in the air, ready to be placed on a van and taken to a municipal depot. I explained to the policeman why I had left the car there, and he said, "Put it down, he is a Roma fan like us, sorry mate."

Having escaped a hefty fine, I picked up Maurizio and Rossella and went to the Stadio Olimpico. During the match Roma scored and we were all jumping and shouting and hugging, and Maurizio is a tall strong man.

In the evening I flew back to the UK, but during the night, I could not go to sleep because of a pain in my chest and I went to A&E. The X ray showed I had two cracked ribs. When I mentioned it to Maurizio he replied, "If you are a puff don't come to football matches". From then on when we went to matches I made sure that Rossella was sitting between myself and Maurizio.

On another occasion, my wife Jo, knowing I gave lessons in my flat and occasionally I would not have enough chairs, presented me with a plastic garden chair. Jo and I have separated many years ago, but we are on friendly terms. I tried to refuse it because I did not know where to store it and I only have a communal garden, to no avail. I found a place for it and forgot about it. One day my student Janet, whom I had met in the Grange Theatre, told me she was going to increase sales in a charity shop in Coalville, forty miles from Walsall, and did I have anything for her. Among other things I gave her THE chair. A few days later Jo asked me where the chair was. I told her that by now would be used somewhere in Coalville. She did not like that I had given away her present to me, even if it was for charitable reasons, I told her I would buy one exactly the same, but she wanted me to have THE chair. I called Janet and asked for the phone number of the charity shop and she could not understand why I had to go to Coalville when I could buy another chair exactly the same in Walsall for a few pounds. Anyway, the chair had not been sold. It was a beautiful sunny day and I took it as a trip in the countryside. When I arrived in Coalville I could not park my car near the charity shop because it was situated in a shopping area, so I carried on and left the car in a street nearby. When I entered the charity shop I was met with giggles because the staff knew I had come from Walsall to get back my chair while I could have bought locally, but I did not care, it was mission accomplished!! I started walking towards my car, but I could not remember where I had left it, so I asked for directions to a lady who was walking towards me. She told me to follow her, then noticing THE chair she asked me, "Have you come for the football match?"

I did not have the courage to tell her the truth, so I replied, "Oh yes, I always take a chair with me in case the match is sold out." By the way Coalville plays football in the same Evo Stick league as my local club, Rushall Olympic, and I have watched Coalville play in Walsall.

As luck wanted my car was in the same road as the football stadium, so when I turned towards it I did not arise any suspicion in the lady. As soon as she was out of sight I put the chair into the car and drove toward an Italian restaurant where I had an excellent lunch. But this is not the end of the story.

When I was back in Walsall Jo admitted that THE chair was not ideal for my flat and told me to give it to our son Marco, I immediately went to Marco's home and when he opened the door I said, "Marco I heard on the grapevine that you needed a garden chair, here it is one." I put it in his arms and turned back and I could hear him saying "But dad.........."

On one occasion I had a special present. A few years ago, my daughter Laura gave me as a birthday present a ride in a Ferrari formula one car and I was over the moon. Having chosen the day and the race track, I went. I had a couple of circuits with a Ferrari instructor who showed me how to change gears using a lever on the steering wheel, on the left if I wanted to accelerate and, on the right, if I wanted to slow down. My worry was to not make a mistake because it is easy to change gears up instead of down, thus accelerating instead of slowing down. Driving around a bend I noticed a big red cross painted on a wall and I asked the instructor what it was.

'Well you see we do have accidents here, so instead of taking injured people to the nearest hospital, we treat them here.'

My heart sank, but I could not chicken out, it was too late, and my son Christian was there to watch me. I started my hour of driving and I enjoyed it more and more as I gained experience and confidence every lap that went by, and when I really was mastering the gear change my hour finished. My son told me that I went slow the first few laps, but then I went faster and faster all the time. I just wished I had never seen that red cross.

Another incident involves the seating in cinemas and theatres. Years ago, I went to the Prince of Wales Theatre in Cannock. There was a show of schoolchildren and only parents and grandparents were in the audience, so that only fifty people were scattered in a four hundred seat theatre. I had ignored the seat allocated to me and I had sat in the middle of an empty row. After a while a lady turned up and showing me her ticket shouted, "Get up, this is my seat!' ignoring that she could have sat anywhere she wanted on that row, but she wanted to sit in HER seat. I jumped in the row behind which was also empty and let her enjoy the seat allocated to her. I admire the British for the stiff upper lip, forming a queue even if there are only two people and so on, but, "This is my seat!" takes the biscuit.

Over many years of going to theatres and cinemas, from London West End to the Midlands, I have developed a strategy: I wait till a couple of minutes before the show starts, and if there still are seats available I go to the ones more comfortable than the one I bought or with a better view. Rarely I had to get up and sit somewhere else because the "owner" of that seat had arrived. A few weeks ago, I went to the local Walsall cinema to watch with a friend "The Guernsey literary and potato peel pie society". At the box office we were warned that nobody else had bought tickets and then she asked, "Where would you like to seat?" I nearly started laughing, then I mumbled something. We were indeed the only two people in the cinema and we sat where we wanted. Before the film started I was half expecting someone to come in and demand those seats.

Another funny incident involved the toilets. Until the latest refurbishment of Birmingham New Street railway station, if the public had to spend a penny he or she had to go to a toilet where a lady collected the 20p entrance fee. I was affected by my usual urge and when in front of the lady I asked, "Is this where I pay and display?"

The lady replied with a smile on her face, 'No Sir, you pay here but display at the end of the corridor.'

About ten years ago I had not long moved to the flat where I still live, when the Council notified the people living in my area that the mobile company O2 had made a request to erect a mast about 100 metres from my flat. The Council had called a meeting in St. Michael Church Hall, just across the road. I and other residents went, the meeting was chaired by a councillor. I objected that O2 wanted to build the mast next to an electric substation which was supposed to be causing cancer, and at the time it was on the news that a whole town had refused to have a mast erected for the same reason. I also asked why O2 wanted to build the mast since I had an O2 mobile and I did not notice any problem. The reply was "For future reception capacity". I observed that the mast could have been erected in the middle of Park Lime pits where nobody lives, and which is used by walkers, fishermen and the like. But a lady stood up and retorted "But I live there!". At that point I had another idea "Why O2 does not erect the mast in the middle of Coalpool Cemetery, nobody would object because they are already dead there!" My motion was approved and to this day no mast has been erected and the mobile reception is still good, this is a technology mystery.

I had started writing this book with the intention of writing only about curious or funny episode of my life, but I must make an exception for the female vicar Liz, who used to share the Parish duties with Colin. Liz had the voice you can imagine an angel has, sweet and gentle, and I was immediately conscious of her extraordinary charismatic character, as if I could see a halo over her head. Liz had not told me that for many years she had been looking after her disabled husband who was confined to a wheelchair, and apparently, she led a normal life, she even came rambling with me. One day we were in church and after the service she mentioned she had an upset stomach, and I thought nothing about it. A few days later she was diagnosed as having pancreatic cancer which is the only incurable cancer. She used to live within walking distance from St. Michael church and from were I lived, so when she became incapacitated to do her duties as a vicar, I used to pop in her home for a quick visit. It was obvious she was becoming frailer by the day. On one of my visits I told her I was going to Rome and asked her what she would like me to bring back to her. She said she wanted a blessed rosary, I promised I would do my best, but I could not promise to have it blessed by the Pope.

When in Rome I took the small party I was leading to visit the "Abbazia delle tree fontane" or the Abbey of the three fountains, situated where St. Paul was decapitated and his head rolling three times caused three springs to come to life. A church was built on that place and in the same area there is a church built with bricks dating to the fourth century and the abbey where the monks looked after the site and apart from praying manufactured and sold speciality bars of chocolate and liqueurs in their café under the brand "Tre fontane.".

Next to the café there was a souvenir shop run by nuns, I went in and saw rosaries on sale. I explained to the nun who was serving me the wish of Liz, and she called the Abbot to bless the rosary, I also bought a religious calendar. Back in Walsall I went to give Liz the rosary and she loved it, then I gave her the calendar and told her to turn the pages every month till Christmas came. He replied in her suave voice "Antonio I am afraid I will not be here at Christmas" and in saying so she opened a draw and gave me the most precious thing she owned, not jewellery or money, but a picture of herself holding the wheelchair where her husband was sitting, during an audience with Pope Woitilya, and the Pope had signed the picture. Then we prayed together. A couple of weeks later Liz died, I went to her funeral and cremation, and her ashes buried within St. Michael church cemetery, in a way she is still with us.

When I came to the UK thirty years ago nobody wanted to employ me because I was "Too old", in order not to leave too many blanks in my CV, I found employment as a volunteer in a shop called "Health Matters", situated next to the old bus station in Walsall. I was young, fit and two stones lighter, so I looked the part. After an induction I started the job. It consisted of weighing, measuring the height and giving the BMI (Body Mass Index) to the clients who came in. If they were overweight I advised what exercise to do, and what healthy food to eat. The majority of clients were middle aged ladies. I enjoyed working there because I felt I was doing something useful. Then I was offered my first job as a teacher and had to leave. Months later I met in Walsall the manager of

"Health Matters" and she told me "Antonio I wish you could come back because all the ladies want to be measured and weighted by you". Now thirty years later I am overweight and not so fit, so I went to a "Weight Watchers" meeting, just to check if I could be helped in losing weight. And I was weighted, measured and given my BMI index, also given advise on dieting and exercising, no more no less than what I was doing thirty years earlier. At the end of the meeting there was a clapping and cheering session when the lady in charge was announcing how many ounces Tracy or Linda had lost during the week, typical American. I thanked and left.

Do you remember when just arrived from Italy I discarded an empty cigarette packet in Soho and told by a policeman to pick it up or ese? Times have changed and I have become a litter picker, I started by picking litter by hand, the I acquired a professional litter picker. It has become a mania and I am addicted to it, when I can I get a big bin liner and walk within a mile from my flat picking up litter. Over the last few years I must have picked a huge amount of litter. On my walks I have met people who encourage me but offer no help. I do not bring back the litter to my recycling bin because it would fill in within a couple of days but dump the filled bin liner in the bin of neighbours. One day a man came out from his house and asked me what I was doing, I told him I was cleaning the area from litter, including the litter around his home, he offered no help, but only wanted to know if I was dumping my bag in the correct bin! Another day I was walking and litter picking when I met a young couple with a child about ten years of age, and he asked me "Why are you picking litter up?" and I did not know what to answer.

I enjoy doing it, it keeps me outdoors and I feel I am doing something worthwhile for myself and the community. There are fines for people who litters the streets or the countryside, but in some towns like Lichfield are enforced and Lichfield is litter free. Sometimes I meet people who tell me "It is all Mc Donald's fault!". I reply that when you buy a Mc Donald's take away you are not told "Please as soon as you leave the restaurant throw empty cans and wrappers on the floor", on the contrary litter bins are provided inside and outside their restaurant, but the majority of clients still prefer to throw everything on the ground. What really makes me think that some people are nearing madness, is when on my walks I find that dog walkers pick up the mess left by their dogs, put it in some small black bags, then tie the bag on a three branch as if it were a flower, or other times throw the bag in the same spot where they have picked up their dog mess. I remember years ago I was on holiday in Ilfracombe, North Devon, and I was relaxing sitting on a bench in a park. A fellow litter picker appeared and started looking for litter in the rose beds end under bushes, with no success.

After marrying Jo, I moved to Via Vito Bering, where I rented a small flat about 300 yards from my home. It was a new flat in an intensively built area of flats, situated in a small narrow road. I soon had to move because of the arrival of children, so I rented a bigger flat in Via Guido Castelnuovo, still in a narrow road on the ground floor. There were no garages and sometime I had to park a long way away, but it was handy because I could walk to the pick-up point of the Alitalia bus taking me to work at the airport, next to the Basilica of St. Paul Outside the Walls. Then one day I opened the newspaper and there was a one-page advertisement of a company advertising a new residential area on the Via Marco Polo that connected Roma to the seaside town of Ostia. The development was called "Casalpalocco", and it was made of houses with gardens and garages. Half the page of the newspaper showed a picture of Via Guido Castelnuovo and the caption – Somebody builds like this – and the other half showed the picture of Casalpalocco and the caption – We build like this.

I realised that Via Guido Castelnuovo had been chosen as the worst road in Rome. I told the owner I wanted to leave and he offered me to buy the flat at a low price, but after those pictures in the newspaper I had decided to go. I collected my saving and bought a beautiful big flat in Ostia, brand new, with underground garages. It was convenient because my children could walk to school and I could walk to the Alitalia coach pick up point. But it was a flat, not a house with garden. Jo being British wanted a house with garden. I started looking in the Casalpalocco area, but the houses were too expensive.

An Alitalia colleague, Emanuele Blasucci, married to Anna Miles, half British half Italian, took me to see his house in the Infernetto area, opposite Casalpalocco. It was called Infernetto, or little hell because a long time ago, people had cut down trees and slowly burned them, to make cheap coal. From a distance the area looked like a smouldering mass of small mounds, resembling hell. The houses in the area had been built illegally without a building licence, and lacked water and gas mains, no sanitation, and occasionally the local police and enforced the law, bulldozing the unfinished houses. But if the houses had a roof on and families were living in it, they could not do it. There were similar illegal residential areas all over Italy, because of the very slow bureaucracy, see chapter five. Every so often the government would pass a law of "Sanatoria" and all the houses in those areas became legal, but the owners had to pay a fine. Since the land was cheap, the gardens were four times bigger than in Casalpalocco.

I fell in love with the area, sold the flat in Ostia and bought a house in Infernetto. My garden was 1500 square metres big, the house had two kitchens, two living rooms, a garage, and four bedrooms. We used the water from a well for everything except for drinking, but some people drank it. We used bottled gas, and the electricity was not reliable. When I moved the roads were not tarmacked, it was like moving in the wild west. There was a community feeling because all the neighbours helped each other according to their skills. The "Sanatoria" arrived and the roads were tarmacked, we received drinking water, and in front of my house in Via Ponte Gardena, there was a bus stop!! My house was the last but one before open countryside and farms.

I remember the nearest famer telling me "Antonio after I have sold my crops, whatever is left on the ground I turn over to fertilise the land. So, after I have sold my crop everything unsold is yours, but if I catch you in my land earlier, I will shoot you. I remember going to the fields with a wheelbarrow and filling it with watermelons, tomatoes, and vegetables. Then in a small corner I started growing my vegetables, and I never bought any more. One night I was returning from the airport, when I was stopped by Carabinieri at gunpoint. I stopped and showed my ID. Then I asked why I was stopped, they replied "In this villa lives judge zxwy, who has been receiving death threats, so we are here to protect him." So, a judge was living in an illegal area, at that point I had no more fears. If a judge who might have sentenced me to a fine or ordered to bulldoze my house was living by me, I was safe.